Digital Image Processing Applications

Edited by Paulo E. Ambrósio

Published in London, United Kingdom

IntechOpen

Supporting open minds since 2005

Digital Image Processing Applications
http://dx.doi.org/10.5772/intechopen.95685
Edited by Paulo E. Ambrósio

Contributors
Nupur Karmaker, Edgardo Comas, Adrián Stácul, Saúl Manuel Domínguez Nicolás, Randa Khemiri, Soulef Bouaafia, Asma Bahba, Maha Nasr, Fatma Ezahra Sayadi, Jar-Ferr Yang, Wei-Jong Yang, Cheng-Yu Lo, Pau-Choo Chung, Umamaheswari Kumarasamy, G.V. Shrichandran, A. Vedanth Srivatson

First published in London, United Kingdom, 2022 by IntechOpen
IntechOpen is the global imprint of INTECHOPEN LIMITED, registered in England and Wales, registration number: 11086078, 5 Princes Gate Court, London, SW7 2QJ, United Kingdom
Printed in Croatia

British Library Cataloguing-in-Publication Data
A catalogue record for this book is available from the British Library

Additional hard and PDF copies can be obtained from orders@intechopen.com

Digital Image Processing Applications
Edited by Paulo E. Ambrósio
p. cm.
Print ISBN 978-1-83969-794-4
Online ISBN 978-1-83969-795-1
eBook (PDF) ISBN 978-1-83969-796-8

For EU product safety concerns:
IN TECH d.o.o., Prolaz Marije Krucifikse Kozulić 3, 51000 Rijeka, Croatia, info@intechopen.com or visit our website at intechopen.com.

Meet the editor

Paulo E. Ambrósio has a Ph.D. in Medical Sciences from the Medical School of Ribeirão Preto, University of São Paulo (FMRP/USP), Brazil. He is currently an associate professor in the Department of Exact and Technological Sciences, State University of Santa Cruz (UESC); vice-director of the Center for Radiation Sciences and Technology (CPqCTR/UESC); and is a member of the Special Committee on Computing Applied to Health, Brazilian Computer Society. His research interests include applied computing, with emphasis on health and biology, working mainly with pattern recognition, medical imaging, and computational modeling.

Contents

Preface

When we talk about digital image processing, we can refer to a wide variety of techniques, concepts, and applications of different types of processing for different purposes. The very concept of a digital image is broad enough to depict various aspects and elements, for example, a video, photograph, or medical image.

This book provides examples of digital image processing applications and presents recent research on image processing concepts and techniques. Chapter 1 provides a general introduction to applications of image processing in the field of medical physics, presenting different imaging modalities and some of the main contributions of the use of processing techniques to medicine. Chapter 2 compares different techniques used in one of the most fundamental and important steps of the overall digital image processing cycle: binarization. In this step, we try to represent a digital image with characteristic elements that allow the extraction of relevant information from the image for better computational interpretation. Chapter 3 discusses image processing with a dynamic application. The authors present results obtained using a technique for tracking objects in a video sequence. Chapter 4, presents high-performance processing techniques in video processing that aim to gain computational performance. Chapter 5 deals with automated face recognition, presenting promising results in the use of techniques for recognizing occluded faces in an image, for example, when the individual to be recognized is wearing a mask. Finally, Chapter 6 reviews the techniques and concepts used in CT imaging for the purpose of identifying and characterizing lesions for diagnosing cancer.

We hope this book will inspire young researchers to seek out and develop new technical and scientific advances in digital image processing.

Paulo E. Ambrósio
Universidade Estadual de Santa Cruz,
Ilhéus, BA, Brazil

Chapter 1

Digital Image Processing and Its Application for Medical Physics and Biomedical Engineering Area

Nupur Karmaker

Abstract

The proper use of imaging modalities produces an image that aids in the detection of early stage abnormalities such as cancer, the identification of small precise lesions, and the presentation of internal illustration. A high-quality image can help doctors, radiologists, medical physicists, biomedical engineers, and scientists to make important decisions on ameliorate treatment planning that can reduce cancer mortality rates and provide life-saving results. This chapter outlines the features, attributes, and processing techniques of various medical imaging modalities utilized in the fields of radiation therapy and biomedical engineering. This study highlighted the significance of image processing in medical physics and biomedical engineering, characteristics of mammography, computed tomography (CT), ultrasound, magnetic resonance imaging (MRI), and positron emission tomography (PET) images. With their advanced application, various image processing approaches are distinguished. Images are collected through the journal, useful websites, the internet, or other sources. That can help teachers, students, researchers, scientists, and others comprehend and learn how to apply image processing techniques and which techniques will suit which modalities image. This chapter will provide a clear understanding of image processing techniques for medical physics and biomedical engineering participants, as well as an abundance of learning opportunities.

Keywords: mammography, ultrasound, computed tomography, positron emission tomography (PET), magnetic resonance imaging (MRI), image processing techniques, medical physics, biomedical engineering and importance

1. Introduction

Present status of the globe, special issue for the international community in this 21st century struggle against COVID-19 has been taken a tremendous place by the greatest health, economy, education, and food challenges that are denigrating normal process safety lifestyle of human, animal, agriculture, etc. [1]. Simultaneous global emergency situation handled by World Health Organization (WHO), policymakers, research center, institutions, universities, and scientific societies that are still finding affordable and practical solutions for prevention, diagnosis, treatment, and management to abate affected and death rate, manage patients in each stage of the disease control, secure quality and safety for patients, front liners, healthcare workers, and general people by accurate diagnosis kits, respirators, face shields, ventilators, intensive care units (ICUs), personal protective equipment (PPE), medical devices, medicine, and vaccines [2, 3].

COVID-19 disrupted medical services more than half (53%) of the countries for hypertension treatment; 49% for treatment for diabetes and diabetes-related complications; 42% for cancer treatment, 31% for cardiovascular emergencies, and almost two-thirds (63%) for rehabilitation services [4].

In a devastating unexpected situation of COVID-19 hampered and increased higher risk for cancer patients, doctors, medical physicists, nurses, and other staff to ensure safe, sanitization, segregation, face/body shielding maintain social distance, and prepare radiotherapy infrastructures [5]. Clinical medical physicists approach who are working clinical services, education, informatics, equipment performance evaluation, quality assurance, treatment planning, brachytherapy, in vivo dosimetry, motion management, etc. mitigate infection risk to staff [6, 7]. Medical physicists formulated certain strategies based on published evidence to help to formulate their own protocols to carry out planning and treatment considering time, distance, and shielding it remains unchanged for COVID-19 [8].

Biomedical engineers are preserving life in different ways to fortify during COVID-19 pandemic for healthcare infrastructure, imaging modalities, medical equipment designed to avail contain the SARS-CoV-2 virus responsible for causing COVID-19 infections, rapid and reliable test kits, face mask, face shield, ventilator, oximeter, better nasal swabs, 3D printing, artificial intelligence applications, and vaccine development [9, 10].

On the other hand, human history has high death rate for some diseases per year. According to WHO report in 2019, the top 10 causes of death accounted for 55% of the 55.4 million deaths worldwide [11]. Leading causes of death globally are illustrated below (**Figure 1**).

The two fields of human health and medical imaging are inextricably linked one another. The use of high-quality imaging modalities is essential for accurate diagnosis [12]. Early detection and accurate assessment of lesions are the goals of various image modalities. The properties of imaging modalities and methodologies contribute to produce an image for clinical visibility [13]. The use of digital processing is a powerful tool to quickly analyze enhanced/intensified images [14]. Nowadays

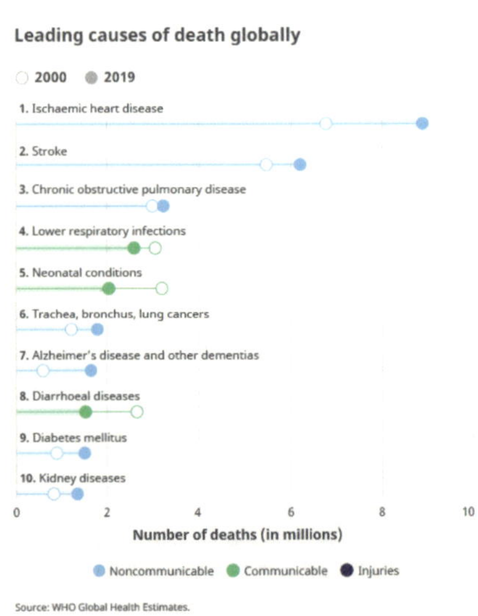

Figure 1.
Leading causes of death globally [11].

artificial neural networks and deep learning applied for better understanding medical image analysis [15].

Significant image processing can assist to provide accurate anatomical information that can always play a vital role in early-stage detection, reducing death rates, and take better treatment decisions [16].

The goal of this empirical study is to show that there is a significant link between medical physics and biomedical engineering with digital image processing, as well as how to apply image processing techniques in this area and what types of benefits can be obtained. So, this is the fundamental concern for introducing the medical physics and biomedical engineering working field, what sorts of modalities are used here for diagnosis and treatment reasons, what essential features can be seen in various modalities images, and which image processing techniques are preferred.

2. Medical physics

The application of physics to medicine is known as medical physics which encompasses therapeutic radiological physics, medical, nuclear physics, and medical health physics [17]. A fundamental component of medical physics is the requirement for broad imaging facilities and accurate explanations [16]. The journey of medical physics and imaging began with the discovery of X-ray that is known as medicine in radiation [18]. Radiation therapy (RT) was first used to treat cancer over a century ago. Since then, enormous progress has been made to improve the effectiveness of this modality and minimize side effects [19]. Radiation therapy is a form of radiation medicine that consists of external beam radiation therapy and brachytherapy that is used to treat a variety of cancer cases. Radiation therapy (also called radiotherapy) is a cancer treatment that uses high doses of radiation to kill cancer cells and shrink tumors [20].

Various machines have been used to produce radiation beams throughout the history of radiation therapy [21]. High-energy X-ray or electron beams used for cancer treatment that is known as external beam radiation therapy (EBRT) [22]. Brachytherapy is a treatment in which radioactive material is implanted into patient body.

One type of radiation therapy used to treat cancer is brachytherapy or internal radiation therapy [23].

Stereotactic irradiation, total body irradiation, total skin electron irradiation, intraoperative radiotherapy, endocavitary rectal irradiation, conformal radiotherapy, image guided radiotherapy, adaptive radiotherapy, respiratory gated radiotherapy, and PET/CT scanners and PET/CT image fusion are some special techniques use for treated cancer to achieve better outcome [24].

2.1 Importance of digital image processing: Medical physics in radiation therapy

Medical imaging, tumor localization, skin reference marks, treatment planning, virtual simulation are key parts of radiation treatment [25].

Medical diagnosis for detection, staging, grading, treatment planning before radiation therapy, treatment guidance and verification, evaluation of response to therapy, and treatment follow-up is involved with imaging of tumors and surrounding normal tissues [26].

2.1.1 Tumor localization

In oncology, benign, pre-malignant, and malignant tumors are the most prevalent forms. Early imaging techniques aid in the reduction of cancer-related morbidity. Pre-processing, segmentation, and morphological operation are the three stages of tumor image processing [27]. The goal of this image processing is always to determine tumor location [28]. The main concern of segmentation, detection, and extraction of tumor area from imaging modalities images that helps to perform radiologists or clinical experts for treatment planning [29].

2.1.2 Treatment planning

Treatment planning is a computerized procedure that employs a variety of technologies to update treatment outcomes [30]. Image datasets are required by treatment planning systems in order to construct a detailed plan for each beamline route for delivering radiation. The complex programming for multi-leaf collimator (MLC) leaf is sequencing to shape the beam around critical structures during dose delivery [31]. From the initial characterization of tumor volumes through the development of digitally reconstructed radiographs for patient treatment setup and treatment verification, medical images such as CT images are used in the treatment planning process. CT enables tumor imaging as well as the reconstruction of three-dimensional (3D) anatomical information, which is then utilized to create patient models with all of the relevant anatomic, geometric, and electron density data. CT has become the method of choice for 3D treatment planning due to these characteristics, as well as its widespread availability and inexpensive cost [32].

2.1.3 Virtual simulation

The virtual simulator is a software program that helps with the geometric component of 3D radiation treatment planning [33].

After completion of treatment planning, the patient is directly placed at the LINAC. The actual position is registered by the LINAC-based imaging units [34].

It is obvious that without a high-quality image, all radiation treatments will proceed incorrectly, potentially increasing cancer mortality. As a result, image processing is becoming increasingly important in radiation oncology.

3. Biomedical engineering

The application of engineering ideas and design concepts to medicine and biology for healthcare reasons is known as biomedical engineering (BME) or medical engineering (e.g., diagnostic or therapeutic) [35]. BME's areas of expertise include bioinstrumentation, biomaterials, biomechanics, cell, tissue, and genetic engineering, clinical engineering, medical imaging, orthopedic, and rehabilitation engineering [36].

3.1 Importance of digital image processing in biomedical engineering

The concern of BME is the acquisition of images for diagnostic and therapeutic applications where use advanced sensors and computer technology [37]. A set of anatomical information structures provide by a biomedical images helps to investigate and visualize for treatment [38]. Accurate implant, prepare the biomedical device, joint, and other organ replacement is required good quality images.

3.1.1 Bioinformatics

The growing usage of medical equipment has resulted in a tremendous amount of data being generated, including image data. Bioinformatics solutions give an effective way to picture data processing in order to recover information of interest and combine several data sources for knowledge extraction; additionally, image processing techniques aid scientists and physicians in diagnosis and treatment [39]. Some bioimage informatics are mentioned here: high-throughput and high-content analysis of cellular phenotypes, Atlas building for model organisms, understanding the dynamic processes in cells and living organisms, joint analysis using both bioimage informatics and other bioinformatics methods [40].

3.1.2 Biomechanics

Medical imaging is crucial in the construction of anatomically realistic, cutting-edge finite element models that can be employed in biomechanical research [41]. In the discipline of biomechanics, Digital Image Correlation (DIC) is being used. However, because DIC is based on a number of key assumptions, it necessitates rigorous optimization to provide accurate and precise findings [42].

3.1.3 Biomaterial and tissue engineering

Repair, replacement, restoration of hard and soft tissues continue to grow as the population ages using biomaterials require to investigate internal anatomy so imaging has been taken a crucial role in this field [43].

3.1.4 Genetic engineering

Molecular imaging offers a novel way to observe cellular and molecular phenomena such as cell survival, migration, proliferation, and even differentiation at the whole-organism level without causing harm. For monitoring cell grafts in vivo, a variety of imaging methods and methodologies used for investigating the condition [43].

3.1.5 Biomedical optics

Techniques, equipment, instruments, probes, computer algorithms and software, and clinical trials make up the discipline of biomedical optical imaging [44]. Without medical imaging modalities, image processing medical physics and biomedical engineering is impossible.

4. Imaging modalities for cancer diagnosis

Different types of imaging modalities are utilized in diagnosis. How to get an image from modalities is a popular inquiry for the audience. Some imaging modalities are given below:

4.1 Mammography

One of the most frequent diagnostics for detecting breast tissue abnormalities is mammography, which uses X-rays to create images of the breast that is known as a mammogram [45]. The two-dimensional image that relies on the identification of morphologic findings for breast cancer these findings include masses, grouped calcifications, asymmetries, and areas of architectural distortion. Spot compression, magnification, rolling, extended views, and genuine lateral views are some of the diagnostic mammographic views that can be used to describe and locate abnormalities [46]. When a high-energy X-ray photon with a low dose interacts with tissue, the photon is attenuated. The reconstruction method captures and images changes in attenuation. In terms of identifying cancer, it has a high specificity sensitivity and temporal response of a portable gadget (about 1 minute). When employing mammography, good resolution means higher accuracy in thick breasts. The number of false-positive predictions is considerable. When compared to CT and MRI, the contrast is poor [47].

Worldwide breast cancer screening programs, digital mammography (DM) use as a standard imaging technique. The primary benefit of DBT is that it provides depth information about the breast, allowing for improved imaging of possible concealed lesions and demonstrating a difficult reconstruction procedure to build a pseudo-3D representation of the breast from a small number of projection images [48]. The image quality of digital breast tomosynthesis (DBT) volumes depends greatly on the reconstruction algorithm [49]. DBT images have the acquisition of several low-dose planar X-ray projections of the compressed breast over a limited angular range, which is then reconstructed into a pseudo-3D volume. The inherent challenges of this acquisition approach degrade image quality. The limited angle acquisition gives rise to out-of-plane artifacts and low vertical resolution, the low dose per projection increases the impact of noise, and X-ray scatter decreases contrast. The reconstruction algorithm is one of the main aspects of image creation that could ameliorate these technical drawbacks and therefore can greatly affect the final quality of DBT images [50]. DBT has been demonstrated to help with two-dimensional (2D) mammography breast tissue overlapping concerns. However, contemporary DBT technologies are still limited in comparison to mammography. Statistical image reconstruction (SIR) approaches have the ability to reduce DBT through-plane artifacts, and hence could be utilized to reduce anatomical clutter even more [51].

Galactography can detect a variety of breast abnormalities, including pathological nipple discharge, which is described as bloody, serous, or clear single-orifice nipple discharge [52]. The GL technique is essential for diagnosing and finding intraductal lesions. GL has been shown in several trials to be ineffective in distinguishing benign from malignant tumors [53].

Scintimammography using 99mtc-sestamibi is a non-invasive and painless diagnostic imaging method where a variety of radiopharmaceuticals create planar and tomographic pictures as well as provide information on tumor cell viability and cellularity that is used to detect breast cancer when mammography is inconclusive [54]. In the presence of cancer tissue, the radiopharmaceutical accumulates in the breast, which may be seen clearly in the photographs [55]. It is the most widely used agent for this purpose because of the advantages of 99mTcsestamibi tagging and its great efficiency in detecting carcinomas [56].

4.1.1 Image processing techniques

- Contrast stretching, histogram processing, spatial filtering (mean filter and median filter) [57]

- Adaptive histogram equalization (AHE), brightness preserving bi-histogram equalization (BPBHE), recursive mean separate histogram decomposition (RMSHD), multi-decomposition histogram equalization (MDHE), minimum mean brightness error bi-histogram equalization (MMBEBHE), and adaptive smoothing [58]

- Low pass filtering: Butterworth low pass filter and Gaussian low pass filter. High pass filtering: ideal high pass filter and Butterworth high pass filter [58]

- Enhancement based upon wavelet transform and morphology, morphological operations (enhancement of image using multi-scale morphology) [59]
- Direct contrast enhancement techniques [60]
- Adaptive neighborhood contrast enhancement [61]
- Removal of noise using wiener function [62]
- An intuitionistic fuzzification scheme based on the optimization of intuitionistic fuzzy entropy and contrast limited adaptive histogram equalization (CLAHE) [63]
- Mammogram enhancement, non-subsampled pyramid (NSP), low pass filter (LPF), high pass filter (HPF), directional filter bank (DFB), 2D-directional edge filter (HTDE), combining directional and scale features, adaptive histogram equalization (AHE), one-dimensional spatial profile of difference of Gaussian and HTDE filter, detection of microcalcification (MC) [64, 65]

4.2 Ultrasound

A hand-held transducer transmits and receives pulsed acoustic waves, which are used in medical ultrasound imaging. This is a well-established technique that is widely used throughout the world. Its benefits include cost-effectiveness, flexibility, and the absence of ionizing radiation [66]. Generally, the morphology, orientation, internal structure, and margins of lesions from multiple planes with a high resolution both in predominantly fatty breasts and dense, glandular structures find out from ultrasound [67]. Ultrasound electrography, contrast-enhanced ultrasound, three-dimensional ultrasound, automated breast sonography, computer-aided detection for breast ultrasound use for better outcome of image quality [68].

The biggest disadvantage of ultrasound is its restricted penetration, which is due to the fact that sound waves cannot pass through bone or air, limiting its usage in the brain, lungs, and abdominal region [69].

4.2.1 Image processing techniques

- Modern beamforming techniques, dynamically focused transmission and reception, apodization, limited diffraction beams, pulse compression, compounding, spatial compounding, frequency compounding, strain compounding, harmonic imaging, pulse inversion, filtering, adaptive filters, anisotropic diffusion, wavelets, and deconvolution [70]
- Gray-level normalization, image fuzzification, and fuzzy histogram computation, histogram partitioning and equalization, and image defuzzification [71]
- Contrast limited adaptive histogram equalization (CLAHE) [72] block size, histogram bins, max slope, 3D discrete wavelet transform (3D DWT), wavelet thresholding, and bilateral filter [73]

4.3 CT

The CT scanner displays several slices of bodily tissues in various directions [74]. Due to more informative CT images so it is more effective than X-ray [75].

The resolution, noise, and contrast are the three key elements that influence image quality [76]. Contrast materials are frequently injected into the body during CT scans to improve visibility of certain organs, blood arteries, or tissues by increasing contrast between these locations and surrounding structures in CT images. Contrast enhanced CT (CECT) is a technique that provides useful anatomical information that is not acquired by standard non-enhanced CT (NECT) imaging [77]. Modern micro-CT- and X-ray-based scanners allow the acquisition of three-dimensional (3-D) images of core samples with a resolution as fine as 0.1 μm per voxel these images can be used to construct 3-D digital models of core samples in extremely fine detail [78].

4.3.1 Image processing techniques

- Noise filter, watershed segmentation, thresholding, image acquisition, and image pre-processing (smoothing, enhancement, image segmentation, feature extraction, and classification) [79]
- Data analyze and interpretations: histogram, particles analyze, and profile plot [80]

4.4 MRI

Magnetic resonance imaging (MRI) is a noninvasive imaging tool for examining anatomic features, physiological functions, and tissue molecular composition [81]. MRI is known as a non-invasive, radiation-free imaging technology for detecting and diagnosing small lesions, with significant implications for various kinds of cancer diagnosis, prognosis, and treatment [82].

4.4.1 Image processing techniques

- Histogram equalization techniques, typical histogram equalization (HE), brightness preserving bi-histogram equalization (BBHE), recursive mean separated histogram equalization (RMSHE), and dynamic histogram equalization (DHE) [83]
- Dynamic block coding [84]
- Median filter, Wiener filter [85]
- Local area histogram equalization (LAHE) [86]

4.5 Positron emission tomography (PET)

PET and combined PET/computed tomography (CT) is increasingly used for oncologic imaging [87]. Fluorodeoxyglucose (FDG) PET demonstrates abnormal metabolic features associated with malignancy that often precedes morphologic findings demonstrated with anatomic imaging [88]. Combined PET/CT systems are increasingly available and currently account for almost all of the new whole-body PET installations [89]. In these systems, the CT and PET images are fused and provide combined anatomic and physiologic imaging [90]. Typically, the CT portion is used to provide attenuation correction as well as an anatomic correlation for the PET imaging component [91]. This modality allows more precise anatomic localization of PET abnormalities and in general has been shown to improve diagnostic accuracy compared with FDG PET alone [92].

4.5.1 Image processing techniques

- Gauss filter, high order derivatives of Gauss filter [93]
- Shock filter, Bettahar's image filtering model, speckle reducing anisotropic diffusion [94]
- Coherence enhancing filter [95]
- Stationary wavelet transform (SWT) and Discrete Wavelet Transform (DWT) [96]

5. Limitation

This chapter has lots of information on the role of digital image processing in medical physics and biomedical engineering areas that can be a little bit confused for the reader. It was challenging to place image processing in this area and popular in the non-medical environment.

6. Future direction

This chapter enriches by multi-disciplinary research area. This is offering lots of research information for the audience. The audience can be able to carry on individual research based on each topic.

7. Conclusion

Overview of medical imaging with their modalities, application, and outcome stated here. The combination of medical physics and biomedical engineering area is a vast and worldwide recognized field. Both areas fight against global health challenges. History from human, this is the main concern for ensuring safety for human, animal, plant, and other living matter. In this planet suffers a lot in various time hit living system but always these areas highly contributing lifesaving. This chapter is given an inspirational message for the young because lots of do wait for their contribution to change the future world. Especially women can highly contribute to gynecological health challenges because all corners of the cannot be developed in this area equally. So, some conservative environment always prefers women for gynecological challenges. This chapter highlighted to significance role of image and image processing for this area, imaging modalities for various images, image processing techniques. Various kinds of image processing techniques are mentioned here for growing creative interests.

Acknowledgements

Thanks to all who are associated and contributed to this book.

Conflict of interest

Not Applicable

Learning outcomes

The reader will be able

- to expatiate the role of medical physics and biomedical engineering area
- to identify the known image of image processing
- to characterize various modalities images
- to outline that image processing can contribute to medical science
- to apply image processing techniques
- to find out lots of reading materials and exhort to study in this area

Useful learning materials

- https://github.com/sfikas/medical-imaging-datasets
- https://www.cancerimagingarchive.net/primary-data/
- https://datacommons.cancer.gov/repository/imaging-data-commons
- https://nucmedicine.iaea.org/home

Mammography

- https://www.rsna.org/education
- http://www.sprawls.org/resources/MAMMO/module.htm
- https://venturebeat.com/2019/03/21/nyu-open-sources-breast-cancer-screening-model-trained-on-over-200000-mammography-exams/
- http://www.eng.usf.edu/cvprg/Mammography/Database.html

Ultrasound

- https://www.ultrasoundtraining.com.au/resources/free-ultrasound-e-books/
- https://www.mathworks.com/matlabcentral/answers/524385-ultrasound-image-processing-roi-contrast-in-db
- http://www.med.umich.edu/dipl/research.html

CT

- http://www.sprawls.org/resources/CTIMG/module.htm
- https://www.kaggle.com/kmader/siim-medical-images

MRI

- https://radiology.ucsf.edu/research/labs/quantitative-image-processing_a#accordion-ct-angiography
- https://uwaterloo.ca/vision-image-processing-lab/research-topics
- https://www.aylward.org/notes/open-access-medical-image-repositories

PET

- https://www.petimagingresources.com/
- https://cai2r.net/resources/pet-mr-dataset/

SPECT

- http://www.people.vcu.edu/~mhcrosthwait/clrs322/SPECTimagingparameters.html

Radiology organizations

- https://en.wikipedia.org/wiki/Category:Radiology_organizations

Organization/society of medical physics

- The American Association of Physicists in Medicine (AAPM)
- https://www.aapm.org/
- International Organization for Medical Physics (IOMP)
- https://www.iomp.org/
- Institute of Physics and Engineering in Medicine (IPEM)
- https://www.ipem.ac.uk/
- European Federation of Organizations For Medical Physics (EFOMP)
- https://www.efomp.org/
- Australasian College of Physical Scientists and Engineers in Medicine (ACPSEM)
- https://www.acpsem.org.au/Home
- Asia-Oceania Federation of Organizations for Medical Physics
- https://afomp.org/
- Middle East Federation of Medical Physics (MEFOMP)

- https://www.mefomp.com/
- South East Asian Federation of Organizations for Medical Physics (SEAFOMP)
- http://seafomp.org/home/

Organization/society of biomedical engineering

- IUPESM
- https://2018.iupesm.org/about/
- IFMBE
- https://ifmbe.org/
- https://guides.libraries.psu.edu/c.php?g=318448&p=2258484
- https://guides.library.uab.edu/c.php?g=386396&p=2621393

Useful Video Links

Mammography

- https://www.youtube.com/watch?v=B_LASa80I8I
- https://www.youtube.com/watch?v=FJl_yf5Au68
- https://www.youtube.com/watch?v=H3wrzoV_Ksk
- https://www.itnonline.com/videos/video-how-contrast-enhanced-mammography-will-impact-breast-imaging
- https://www.youtube.com/watch?v=WJKhehpFxow

Ultrasound

- https://www.youtube.com/watch?v=X8ab6NAIV5I
- https://www.youtube.com/watch?v=b1Eh4a1umdw
- https://www.youtube.com/watch?v=4aXEmVCf9HM
- https://www.youtube.com/watch?v=hI51xJ0qxSk
- https://www.youtube.com/watch?v=VSjTK_R8e3A

CT

- https://www.youtube.com/watch?v=l9swbAtRRbg
- https://www.youtube.com/watch?v=bgjkJfBHKxg

- https://www.youtube.com/watch?v=wdY9gcjVsNY
- https://www.youtube.com/watch?v=9eeiKhyysLU
- https://www.youtube.com/watch?v=UeFRo7uALhM

MRI

- https://www.youtube.com/watch?v=nFkBhUYynUw
- https://www.youtube.com/watch?v=akuQWr8q9Qs
- https://www.youtube.com/watch?v=G2YsuVzg-Gg
- https://www.youtube.com/watch?v=mBAIWAyNdz0
- https://www.youtube.com/watch?v=ur6pi3L98kk

PET

- https://www.youtube.com/watch?v=k2jnSmpHqzg
- https://www.youtube.com/watch?v=GHLBcCv4rqk
- https://www.youtube.com/watch?v=nnS0YPWuwLY
- https://www.youtube.com/watch?v=64ALTpmtxUw

Author details

Nupur Karmaker
Medial Physics and Biomedical Engineering (MPBME), Gono Bishwabidyalay (University), Dhaka, Bangladesh

*Address all correspondence to: moonnkbme@gmail.com: nupurmpbme@gmail.com

References

[1] Rahul PK, Disha F, Sneha PK, Brayal D. Knowledge and understanding among medical imaging professionals in India during the rapid rise of the Covid-19 pandemic. Health and Technology. 2020;**10**(8):1-6. DOI: 10.1007/s12553-020-00437-2

[2] Andellini M, De SS, Nocchi F, Bassanelli E. Clinical needs and technical requirements for ventilators for COVID-19 treatment critical patients: An evidence-based comparison for adult and pediatric age. Health and Technology. 2020;**10**:1403-1411. DOI: 10.1007/s12553-020-00467-w

[3] Leandro P, Davide P, Alessia M. The inadequacy of regulatory frameworks in time of crisis and in low-resource settings: Personal protective equipment and COVID-19. Health and Technology. 2020;**10**(1):1375-1383. DOI: 10.1007/s12553-020-00429-2

[4] World Health Organization (WHO). COVID-19 Significantly Impacts Health Services for Noncommunicable Diseases. Available from: https://www.who.int/news-room/detail/01-06-2020-covid-19-significantly-impacts-health-services-for-noncommunicable-diseases [Accessed: 25 August 2021]

[5] Supratik S, Saranga PH, Mayuri N, Bimugdha G. Medical physics internship during covid-19 pandemic—What we lost and gained. Asian Pacific Journal of Cancer Care. 2020;**5**(S1):191-193. DOI: 10.31557/apjcc.2020.5.S1.191-193

[6] Arash D, Hossein L, Reza T, Rao K. Mitigating disruptions, and scalability of radiation oncology physics work during the COVID-19 pandemic. Journal of Applied Clinical Medical Physics. American Association of Physicists in Medicine. May 2020. DOI: 10.1002/acm2.12896

[7] May W, Tomas K, Matthew S, Richard D. COVID-19 pandemic planning: Considerations for radiation oncology medical physics. Physical and Engineering Sciences in Medicine. Rapid Communication. 2020;**43**(2):473-480. DOI: 10.1007/s13246-020-00869-0

[8] Yadav B, Sarma G, Barthakur M, Goswami P, Goswami S. Managing radiotherapy practice during coronavirus disease 2019 pandemic: Medical physicist's perspective. Journal of Radiation and Cancer Research. January-March 2020;**11**(1):38. DOI: 10.4103/jrcr.jrcr_16_20

[9] Ala Ş, Ayşe Nur T, Mohammad BA, Mohammad AM, Pınar YH. Role of biomedical engineering during COVID-19 pandemic. Natural and Applied Sciences Journal. 2020;**3**(1):1-16. DOI: 10.38061/idunas.754344

[10] Futurity. 4 Ways Engineers Aim to Save Lives during COVID-19. Available from: https://www.futurity.org/covid-19-engineers-2341552/ [Accessed: 27 July 2021]

[11] World Health Organization (WHO). The Top 10 Causes of Death. 9 December 2020. Available from: https://www.who.int/news-room/fact-sheets/detail/the-top-10-causes-of-death [Accessed: 27 July 2021]

[12] Jacob VD. Radiation oncology medical physics resources for working, teaching, and learning. The Modern Technology of Radiation Oncology. Chapter 16, Vol 3. 1st edition. 2018. pp. 512-514. ISBN: 9781930524576

[13] Perry S. Effective physics knowledge for diagnostic radiologists. The universal image characteristics that affect visibility. Medical Physics International Journal. 2019;**7**(3):261. Available from: http://www.mpijournal.org/pdf/2019-03/MPI-2019-03-p257.pdf

[14] Shaik N. A review on image processing applications in medical field.

Research Journal of Pharmacy and Technology. 2017;**10**(10):3456-3460. DOI: 10.5958/0974-360X.2017.00644.8

[15] Muralikrishna P. Medical image analysis based on deep learning approach. Multimedia Tools and Applications. 2021;**80**:24365-24398. DOI: 10.1007/s11042-021-10707-4. Available from: https://doi.org/10.1007/s11042-021-10707-4

[16] Rama Devi O, Chitra Meghana MS, Jeevana Shruti K. Medical image processing—An overview. International Journal of Innovations in Engineering and Technology. 2016;**7**(3):362-364. Available from: http://ijiet.com/wp-content/uploads/2017/01/54.pdf

[17] Tsair-Fwu L, Jack Y. Radiation oncology and medical physics. BioMed Research International. 2015;**2015**: 297158. DOI: 10.1155/2015/297158. Available from: http://dx.doi.org/10.1155/2015/297158

[18] Amy B. Hershey Pa. The history of radiation use in medicine. Journal of Vascular Surgery. Published 27 September 2010;**53**(1):3S-5S. DOI: 10.1016/j.jvs.2010.07.024. Available from: https://doi.org/10.1016/j.jvs.2010.07.024

[19] Rajamanickam B. Cancer and radiation therapy: Current advances and future directions. International Journal of Medical Sciences. 2012;**9**(3):193-199. DOI: 10.7150/ijms.3635

[20] Timur M. Radiation Therapy Techniques in Cancer Treatment. Available from: https://www.uptodate.com/contents/radiation-therapy-techniques-in-cancer-treatment [Accessed: 31 August 2021]

[21] National Cancer Institute. External Beam Radiation Therapy for Cancer. Available from: https://www.cancer.gov/about-cancer/treatment/types/radiation-therapy/external-beam [Accessed: 1 September 2021]

[22] Patrick NM, Colin GO. The Physics & Technology of Radiation Therapy. 2nd ed. Medical Physics Publishing; 2018. pp. 9-1-9-2. Available from: https://www.medicalphysics.org/documents/Mcdermott2_ch9.pdf

[23] Brachytherapy. Mayo Clinic. Available from: https://www.mayoclinic.org/tests-procedures/brachytherapy/about/pac-20385159 [Accessed: 1 September 2021]

[24] Podgorsak EB, Podgorsak MB. Radiation Oncology Physics: A Handbook for Teachers and Students. International Atomic Energy Agency. Vienna: IAEA Publication; 2005; 505-545. ISBN: 92-0-107304-6. DOI: 10.1038/sj.bjc.6604224

[25] Radiation Therapy Treatment Process. Available from: https://images.slideplayer.com/24/7358130/slides/slide_32.jpg [Accessed: 20 Nov 2021]

[26] Eva FA, Elisabeth K. Medical imaging for improved tumour characterization, delineation and treatment verification. Acta Oncologica. 2002;**41**(7-8):604-614. DOI: 10.1080/028418602321028201

[27] Ed-Edily M. Tumor detection in medical imaging: A survey. International Journal of Advanced Information Technology. 2014;**4**(1): 21-23. DOI: 10.5121/ijait.2014.4103

[28] Nilesh BB, Arun KR, Har PT. Image analysis for MRI based brain tumor detection and feature extraction using biologically inspired BWT and SVM. International Journal of Biomedical Imaging. 2017;**2017**:2-3. DOI: 10.1155/2017/9749108

[29] Zahid U. Critical analysis of brain magnetic resonance images tumor detection and classification techniques. International Journal of Advanced

Computer Science and Applications. 2020;**11**(1):453-456. DOI: 10.14569/IJACSA.2020.0110156

[30] Christian RH, Wouter C. Radiotherapy treatment planning study guidelines (RATING): A framework for setting up and reporting on scientific treatment planning studies. Radiotherapy and Oncology. Elsevier B.V. Available online 22 September 2020;**153**:68-70. DOI: 10.1016/j.radonc.2020.09.033

[31] Fornell D. An Introduction to Current Radiation Therapy Treatment Planning Systems. Imaging Technology News. Feature: Treatment Planning. 08 July 2013. Available from: https://www.itnonline.com/article/introduction-current-radiation-therapy-treatment-planning-systems [Accessed: 20 August 2021]

[32] Mohammad R. CT images and radiotherapy treatment planning of patients with breast cancer: A dataset. Data in Brief. Elsevier Inc.; August 2017;**13**:390-394. DOI: 10.1016/j.dib.2017.06.002

[33] George WS. The portable virtual simulator. International Journal of Radiation Oncology Biology Physics. ASTRO Short Communication. 1991;**21**(2):476-480. DOI: 10.1016/0360-3016(91)90799-A

[34] Mirko N, Nils T, Ulrich MC. International CT scanner based virtual simulation of radiotherapy treatment by the PICTOR 3D® system does not increase efficacy in daily routine radiation therapy. nternational Journal of Radiology and Radiation Oncology. 2015;**1**(1):4-6. DOI: 10.17352/ijrro.000003. ISSN: 2640-7566. Available from: https://www.peertechzpublications.com/articles/IJRRO-1-103.php

[35] Biomedical Engineering. 29 August 2021. Available from: https://en.wikipedia.org/wiki/Biomedical_engineering [Accessed: 1 September 2021]

[36] Planning a Career in Biomedical Engineering. UK, Republic of Ireland: IEEE Engineering in Medicine and Biology Student Society. Available from: https://ewh.ieee.org/sb/ukri/embs/embs/careersinbme.html [Accessed: 1 September 2021]

[37] Renukalatha S, Suresh KV. A review on biomedical image analysis. Biomedical Engineering: Applications, Basis and Communications. World Scientific Publishing Co Pte Ltd.; 2018;**30**(3):2-8. DOI: 10.4015/S1016237218300018. ISSN (print): 1016-2372, ISSN (online): 1793-7132

[38] Yousif Mohamed YA, Alqahtani T. Medical Imaging - Principles and Applications. Chapter 05: Research in Medical Imaging Using Image Processing Techniques. In: Yongxia Z. Editor. London, United Kingdom: IntechOpen Limited. 24 June 2019. ISBN 978-1-78923-872-3. Ebook (PDF) ISBN 978-1-78985-724-5. DOI: 10.5772/intechopen.84360 https://www.intechopen.com/chapters/67331

[39] Pietro C, Luciano C. Bioinformatics Solutions for Image Data Processing. Edited by Robert Koprowski Medical and Biological Image Analysis. London: IntechOpen; 2018:55-66. DOI: 10.5772/intechopen.76459

[40] Hanchuan P. Bioimage informatics: A new area of engineering biology. Bioinformatics. Oxford Academic; 2008;**24**(17):1827-1836. DOI: 10.1093/bioinformatics/btn346

[41] Galbusera F, Cina A. Image-based biomechanical models of the musculoskeletal system. European Radiology Experimental. 2020;**4**:2-13. DOI: 10.1186/s41747-020-00172-3

[42] Marco P, Tommaso MB. Use of digital image correlation to investigate the biomechanics of the vertebra. Journal of Mechanics in Medicine and Biology. 2015;**15**(2):1540004.

DOI: 10.1142/S0219519415400047. Available from: https://www.worldscientific.com/doi/abs/10.1142/S0219519415400047

[43] Cho IK, Wang S. Genetic engineered molecular imaging probes for applications in cell therapy: Emphasis on MRI approach. American Journal of Nuclear Medicine and Molecular Imaging. 2016;**6**(5):234-261

[44] Hebden JC, Boas DA. Topics in biomedical optics: Introduction. Applied Optics. 2003;**42**(16):2869-2870. Available from: https://www.researchgate.net/publication/5460647

[45] Gilbert FJ, Pinker-Domenig K. Diagnosis and Staging of Breast Cancer: When and How to Use Mammography, Tomosynthesis, Ultrasound, Contrast-Enhanced Mammography and Magnetic Resonance Imaging. Available from: https://link.springer.com/chapter/10.1007/978-3-030-11149-6_13

[46] Malet A, Pintoc DG. Breast tomosynthesis reconstruction using TIGRE software tool. Conference Paper. July 2018. DOI:10.1117/12.2317933

[47] Ramya Devi R, Anandhamala GS. Recent trends in medical imaging modalities and challenges for diagnosing breast cancer. Biomedical and Pharmacology Journal. Sept 2018;**11**(3):1649-1658. DOI: 10.13005/bpj/1533

[48] Fiona J, Gilbert, Lorraine T, Ken C. Young Digital breast tomosynthesis (DBT): A review of the evidence for use as a screening tool. Clinical Radiology. Feb 2016;71(2):141-150. DOI: 10.1016/j.crad.2015.11.008

[49] Rodriguez-Ruiz A. New reconstruction algorithm for digital breast tomosynthesis: Better image quality for humans and computers. Acta Radiologica. 2018;**59**(9):1051-1059

[50] Helvie MA. Digital mammography imaging: Breast tomosynthesis and advanced applications. Radiologic Clinics of North America. 2010;**48**(5):917-929. DOI: 10.1016/j.rcl.2010.06.009

[51] Garrett JW, Li Y. Reduced anatomical clutter in digital breast tomosynthesis with statistical iterative reconstruction. Medical Physics. 2018;**45**(5). DOI: 10.1002/mp.12864

[52] Berná-Serna JD, Torres-Alés C. Galactography: An application of the galactogram imaging classification system (GICS). Acta Radiologica. 2009. DOI: 10.3109/02841850903436659

[53] Yücesoy C, Özturk ME. Conventional galactography and MR contrast galactography for diagnosing nipple discharge: Preliminary results. Korean Journal of Radiology. 2008;**9**:426-431. DOI: 10.3348/kjr.2008.9.5.426

[54] Birendra KD, Biswa MB. Role of scintimammography in the diagnosis of breast cancer. Malaysian Journal of Medical Sciences. 2006;**13**(1):52-57

[55] Schillaci O, Danieli R. Scintimammography for the detection of breast cancer. Published online: [Jan 09]. 2014:191-196. DOI: 10.1586/17434440.2.2.191

[56] Moriguchi SM, Antônio de Luca L. Accuracy of 99mTc-sestamibi scintimammography for breast cancer diagnosis. Experimental and Therapeutic Medicine. 2009;**1**:205-209. DOI: 10.3892/etm_00000033

[57] Singh S. Performance Analysis of Mammographic Image Enhancement Techniques for Early Detection of Breast Cancer. Berlin, Heidelberg: Springer-Verlag; 2011. DOI: 10.1007/978-3-642-24037-9_44

[58] Surya Gowri D. A review on mammogram image enhancement techniques for breast cancer detection. In: 2014 International Conference on

Intelligent Computing Applications. 6-7 March 2014; Coimbatore, India: IEEE; 2014. DOI:10.1109/ICICA.2014.19

[59] Chahal JK. A review on various enhancement techniques for mammograms. International Journal of Computers and Applications. 2015; **121**(4):9-12. DOI: 10.5120/21526-4506

[60] Akila K. Mammographic image enhancement using indirect contrast enhancement techniques—A comparative study. Procedia Computer Science. 2015;**47**:255-261. DOI: 10.1016/j.procs.2015.03.205

[61] Kayode AA, Afolabi BS. An explorative survey of image enhancement techniques used in mammography. International Journal of Computer Science. 2015;**12**(1)

[62] Abdallah YMY. Breast cancer detection using image enhancement and segmentation algorithms. Biomedical Research. 2018;**29**(20):3732-3736

[63] Dabass J. Mammogram image enhancement using entropy and CLAHE based intuitionistic fuzzy method. In: 6th International Conference on Signal Processing and Integrated Networks (SPIN). 2019

[64] Anand S. Contrast enhancement of mammograms and microcalcification detection. International Journal of Recent Technology and Engineering. 2019;**8**(4):3926-3932.

[65] Contreras Ortiz SH, Chiua T, Martin D. Ultrasound image enhancement: A review. Biomedical Signal Processing and Control. 2012;**7**(5):419-428. DOI: 10.1016/j.bspc.2012.02.002

[66] Guo R, Lu G. Ultrasound imaging technologies for breast cancer detection and management—A review. Ultrasound in Medicine & Biology. 2018;**44**(1):37-70. DOI: 10.1016/j.ultrasmedbio.2017.09.012

[67] Xian M, Zhang Y. Fully automatic segmentation of breast ultrasound images based on breast characteristics in space and frequency domains. Pattern Recognition. 2015;**48**(2):485-497. DOI: 10.1016/j.patcog.2014.07.026

[68] Slapa RZ. Advantages and disadvantages of 3D ultrasound of thyroid nodules including thin slice volume rendering. Thyroid Research. 2011;**4**(1):1. DOI: 10.1186/1756-6614-4-1

[69] Alexander L. Klibanov. Ultrasound in Radiology: From anatomic, functional, molecular imaging to drug delivery and image-guided therapy. Invest Radiol. 2015 Sep; 50(9): 657-670. DOI: 10.1097/RLI.0000000000000188

[70] Sonia H. Contreras Ortiz Ultrasound image enhancement: A review. Biomedical Signal Processing and Control 2012. Elsevier Ltd. September 2012;**7**(5):419-428. DOI:10.1016/j.bspc.2012.02.002

[71] Taghvatalab S, Karim F. A proposed method for contrast enhancement of breast ultrasound images using FDHE. International Journal of advanced studies in Computer Science and Engineering. 2014;**3**(4):22-27. Available from: https://www.proquest.com/docview/1536118973

[72] Gautam R, Bharti R. Liver ultrasound image enhancement using bilateral filter. International Journal of Engineering & Technical Research. April 2018 ;**8**(4):69-70.Available from: https://www.semanticscholar.org/paper/Liver-Ultrasound-Image-Enhancement-Using-Bilateral-Gautam-Bharti/ef72900fc3012969ec7d32befd915110afd8255f

[73] Singh P. Feature enhancement in medical ultrasound videos using contrast-limited adaptive histogram equalization. Journal of Digital Imaging. Springer. 2019;**33**:273-285. DOI: 10.1007/s10278-019-00211-5

[74] Gajdhane VA. Detection of lung cancer stages on CT scan images by using various image processing techniques. IOSR Journal of Computer Engineering. 2014;**16**(5):28-35. Available from: http://www.iosrjournals.org/

[75] Manickavasagam R. A review on lung nodule detection in CT image using image processing techniques. International Journal of Engineering Research & Technology. 2016;**5**(11):594-596. DOI: 10.17577/IJERTV5IS110352

[76] Priya M, Nagarajan A. Automatic detection and classification of lung carcinoma using image processing techniques in lab view. International Journal of Recent Technology and Engineering. 2020;**8**(5):1216-1219. DOI: DOI:10.35940/ijrte.E5820.018520

[77] Wason JV, Nagarajan A. Image processing techniques for analyzing CT scan images towards the early detection of lung cancer. Bioinformation. 2019;**15**(8):596-599. DOI: 10.6026/97320630015596

[78] Dimililer K, Ugur B. Tumor detection on CT lung images using image enhancement. The Online Journal of Science and Technology. 2017;**7**(1):133-138. Available from: https://www.researchgate.net/publication/328478375_Tumour_Detection_On_Ct_Lung_Images_Using_Image_Enhancement

[79] Logesh Kumar S, Swathy M. Identification of lung cancer cell using watershed segmentation on CT images. Indian Journal of Science and Technology. 2016;**9**(1). DOI: 10.17485/ijst/2016/v9i1/85765

[80] Seleþchi ED, Duliu OG. Image processing and data analysis in computed tomography. In: 7th International Balkan Workshop on Applied Physics. 5-7 July 2006; Romania: Constanþa; 2006

[81] Chan RW, Lau AZ. Core Techniques in Operative Neurosurgery. Encyclopedia of Biomedical Engineering. 2019;**2**:403-405. Available from: https://www.sciencedirect.com/topics/medicine-and-dentistry/magnetic-resonance-imaging. DOI: 10.1016/B978-0-323-52381-3.00074-5

[82] D'Amico NC, Grossi E. A machine learning approach for differentiating malignant from benign enhancing foci on breast MRI. European Radiology Experimental. 2020;**4**:5. DOI: 10.1186/s41747-019-0131-4

[83] Patel S, Bharath KP. Medical image enhancement using histogram processing and feature extraction for cancer classification. Mar 2020: 1-6. Available from: https://arxiv.org/abs/2003.06615

[84] Swamy S. Dynamic block coding for image enhancement for MRI image analysis. International Journal of Engineering Research & Technology. 2019;**8**(10). ISSN: 2278-0181. Available from: https://www.ijert.org/dynamic-block-coding-for-image-enhancement-for-mri-image-analysis

[85] Min A, Kyu MZ. MRI images enhancement and brain tumor segmentation. Advances in Science, Technology and Engineering Systems Journal. 2018;**3**(6):339-346. DOI: 10.25046/aj030642

[86] Sumaya, Vatsa Z. MRI image enhancement. International Journal of Science and Research. 2013;**4**(5): 1757-1758

[87] IAEA Human Health Series. No. 27. PET/CT Atlas on Quality Control and Image Artefacts PET/CT Atlas on Quality Control and Image Artefacts. Vienna: International Atomic Energy Agency; 2014. p. 13. Available from: https://www.iaea.org/publications

ISBN: 978-92-0-101014-8, ISSN: 2075-3772

[88] Abolfazl M. Scott D. Image enhancement of whole-body oncology [18F]-FDG PET scans using deep neural networks to reduce noise. European Journal of Nuclear Medicine and Molecular Imaging. 2021:539-549.DOI: 10.1007/s00259-021-05478-x

[89] Nadig V, Herrmann K. Hybrid total-body pet scanners—current status and future perspectives. European Journal of Nuclear Medicine and Molecular Imaging. 2022;**49**:445-459. DOI: 10.1007/s00259-021-05536-4

[90] Israel O, Keidar Z, Iosilevsky G. The fusion of anatomic and physiologic imaging in the management of patients with cancer. Seminars in Nuclear Medicine. 2001;**31**(3):191-205. DOI: 10.1053/snuc.2001.23525

[91] Griffeth LK. Use of PET/CT scanning in cancer patients: Technical and practical considerations. Proceedings (Baylor University Medical Center). 2005;**18**(4):321-330. DOI: 10.1080/08998280.2005.11928089. ISSN: 0899-8280(Print), 1525-3252 (Online)

[92] Arabi H, Allaf AA. The promise of artificial intelligence and deep learning in PET and SPECT imaging. 2021;**83**: 122-137. DOI: 10.1016/j.ejmp.2021.03.008

[93] Doa'a S, Sami S. Enhancement techniques for positron emission tomography (PET) imaging. 2008. Available from: https://www.researchgate.net/publication/267767112_Enhancement_Techniques_For_Positron_Emission_Tomography_PET_Imaging Accessed 19 February 2022

[94] Mousa A. Adaptive speckle reducing anisotropic diffusion filter for positron emission tomography images based on anatomical prior. In: 24th International Conference on Computer and Technology Applications (ICCTA). 3-5 May 2018. Istanbul, Turkey: IEEE Xplore; 28 June 2018. DOI: 10.1109/CATA.2018.8398682. ISBN: 978-1-5386-6995-2.

[95] Hanan MB, Hala ME, Gamal IS. Enhancement of positron emission tomography (PET) image based on thinning algorithm and shocking filter. Egyptian Computer Science Journal, ECS. 2013;**37**(4):64-79. ISSN: 1110-2586

[96] Fahim S, Hassan G. Combination of wavelet and contourlet transforms for PET and MRI image fusion. In: Artificial intelligence and signal processing (AISP). 25-27 Oct. 2017, Shiraz, Iran. IEEE Xplore; 26 March 2018. pp. 178-183. DOI: 10.1109/aisp.2017.8324077

Chapter 2

Binarization Based on Maximum and Average Gray Values

Saúl Manuel Domínguez Nicolás

Abstract

Many image processing techniques use binarization for object detection in images, where the objects and background are well distinct by their brightness values, where, the threshold level is globally assigned, on the other hand, if it's adaptive, the threshold level is locally calculated. In order to determine the optimal binarization threshold, from an image with the mean gray values and extreme gray values, exchanging the mean gray values relating to automatic analisis for a standard histogram equalization, which can evaluate a wide range of image features, even when the gray values in both the object of interest and background of the image are not uniform.

Keywords: image processing, image are not uniform, mean gray values, extreme gray values, histogram equalization

1. Introduction

In image processing, when one aims to obtain information of interest from image, in order to achieve robust and reliable descriptors. In many image processing algorithms the segmentation technique is widely used to identify regions of input images, which is very important as it may be necessary in the required analysis. Thresholding is the most commonly used technique in image segmentation, and is a binarization method that is used for object detection if background and objects differ by their brightness values. Thresholds values used in a binarization can be chosen manually or automatically. In manual form to find appropriate threshold values it is necessary to perform trial experiments. Automatically selection, combines the image information to get the optimal threshold value. Otsu's algorithm [1] uses image histogram to get the threshold values. There are algorithms based on edges, regions and hybrids, so according to the information used, they define their threshold values. Canny edge detection [2], Sobel edge detection and Laplacian edge detection [3] are algorithms based in the edge information as structures are depicted by edge points. Algorithms suppress the noice in the image to try to find edge pixels. For example, the second derivation information of the image intensity is used by Laplacian edge detection. The gradient magnitude is used in Canny edge detector to find the edge pixels. The pixel intensities are fundamental operations of these algorithms, so discrete pixels make up the detected boundary, hence it can be incomplete or discontinuous. Thus, post-processing techniques like morphological operations is applied to connect generated discontinuities. However, the edges of organs in medical images are not clearly defined, due to noise influence and partial volume effect. Therefore, a pre-processing step is used for the later algorithm base on threshold [4, 5].

Region growing algorithms [6–10] are algorithms that quantify features inside a structure tend to be homogeneous. The grouping is initiated by the similarity of seeds in the desired regions, growing throughout the image considering the properties present in neighboring pixels. Using a seed in the desired región and local criterion an increase in the regions of the input image can be obtained, or through the distribution of seeds in different regions and a global criterion. Nevertheless, due to their reliance on intensity, these algorithms present problems to undo the influence of partial volume effect.

Hybrid algorithms to complete the segmentation use different image properties. Hybrid algorithms are the watershed, which to complete segmentation, use morphological filter, gradient information and image intesity [11–13]. In these algorithms, the gradient magnitude is seen as elevation and as reliefs are considered the gray scale images. Pixels with local maximum gradient define to the watershed lines, which encloses the pixels that define a region of the image. The complete segmentation of an image can be successfully produced through the watershed algorithms. However, when the images are noisy, these algorithms tend to present over-segmentation problems. In knee cartilage image have been reported successful experiments on the segmentation using the marker imposition technique [11]. C-means algorithm [13] is used to avoid the over segmentation problems to improve the performance of watershed algorithm.

At the end of the 90s, some algorithms based in binarization via thresholding [14–17] have been used to obtain the basic mechanical propiertes of materials using the Vickers hardness testing [18–22]. In addition, to eliminate speckles in the segmantation morphological filters have been employed [14–17]. Other segmentation methods have considered to obtain mechanical propiertes in the Vickers hardness testing, such as: template edge matching [23, 24] and dual resolution active contours segmentation [25]. These methods are suitable for indentation images with high contrast and straight edges. Moreover, high computational complexity, multiple parameters specified by the user, and contour detection that may collapse in images with low contrast are challenges in algorithms based on edge and line oriented contour detection [26]. However, in the last three years, have been reported algortihms [27, 28] to detect objects where its edges are not exactly straight lines in low contrast image. These algorithms use thresholding based on the extreme and gray values as binarization creteria, which are distinct from other binarization techniques [14, 17, 24] used to segment similar images.

The purpose of this chapter is to show the reader thresholdization algorithms based on the extreme and gray values as binarization creteria, which are applied to detect objects of interes where theirs edges are not exactly straight lines, and where the gray values in both the object and background of the image are not uniform. In addition to being applied in images with very low contrast, in comparison with the limited capabilities of other algorithms [23, 24, 27–31] to detect objects in this type of images.

This chapter is organized as follows: Section 2 describes image segmentation semi-automatically evaluating maximum and average gray values like binarization creteria. Next, Section 3 describes image segmentation automatically evaluating maximum and average gray values like binarization creteria. Section 4 includes examples of the techniques. Finally, the conclutions are reported in the Section 5.

2. Image segmentation semi-automatically evaluating maximum and average gray values like binarization criteria

At the end of 2018 was reported an algorithm to segment images using maximum and average gray values like binarization criteria [27]. The algorithm's aim was to detect corners, so as to locate the vertices of the object of interest, which is called indentation. Each input image was treated as 2D monochromatic digital image with gray values between 0 and Max, high values corresponding to bright pixels ($Max = white$), and dark pixels having low values ($0 = black$). Each image contains exactly one indentation which is of approximately rhombic shape (see **Figure 1**) whose size, position, and exact orientation in the image are unknown. The indentation is asseumed as a dark region on a brighter background.

Image segmentation of the semiautomatic algorithm, starts with binarization, using the average gray value of the input image as threshold and the difference to the maximum gray value as discriminant criterion. Both the average and the maximum gray value are global characteristics determined from the input image. Denoting the input image by $F = f(x, y), x = x_1, \cdots, x_{\max}; y = y_1, \cdots y_{\max}$, see **Figure 1**, its average gray value is given by $f_{mean} = \frac{1}{x_{\max} y_{\max}} \sum_{x;y} f(x, y)$, and its maximum gray value by $f_{\max} = \max_{x;y} [f(x, y)]$.

Thus, the binarization criterion for every input pixel $p = (x, y) : p$ is considered a pixel of interest whenever $|f(x, y) - f_{\max}| > f_{mean}$.

The result is a binary image $G = g(x, y)$ with $x = x_1, \cdots, x_{\max}, y = y_1, \cdots, y_{\max}$ where each pixel of interes is represented as black, and other pixels are white. Therefore, the indentation region will be a subset of the black pixels. In this type of images to represent the indentation region as black is in coincidence with the fact that this region is dark in the original image.

The first image of the **Figure 2** has an value f_{mean} = 0.3350 and $f_{\max} = 0.5843$, with which is evaluated the binarization criterion for every input pixel of the image. Similar, the second image of the same **Figure 2** presents values of $f_{mean} = 0.3202$ and $f_{\max} = 0.6157$. Finally, the values $f_{mean} = 0.3102$ and $f_{\max} = 0.6057$ are obtained from the third image of **Figure 2**. As a result is the binary image shown in the second column corresponding to each image of the **Figure 2**. However, the binary image there can be many pixels are detected as false positives of the region of interes, as shown in **Figure 2**. Thus, morphological filter is applied to delete these black pixels not belonging to the indentation.

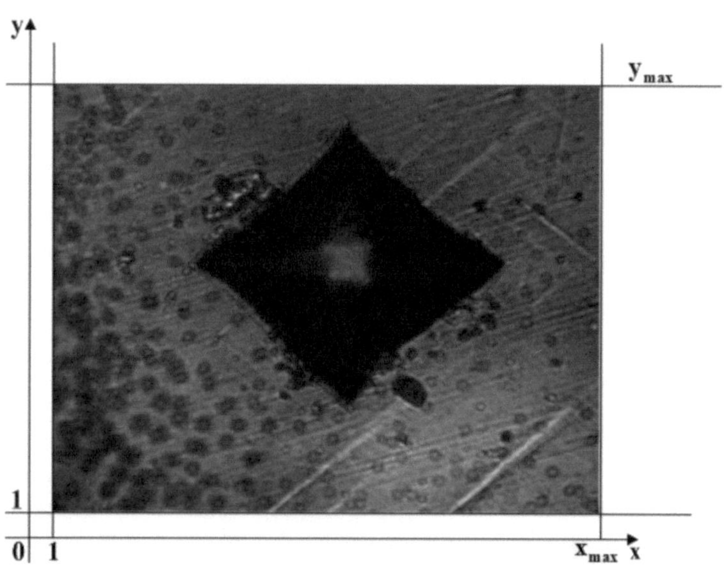

Figure 1.
Example of Indentation image.

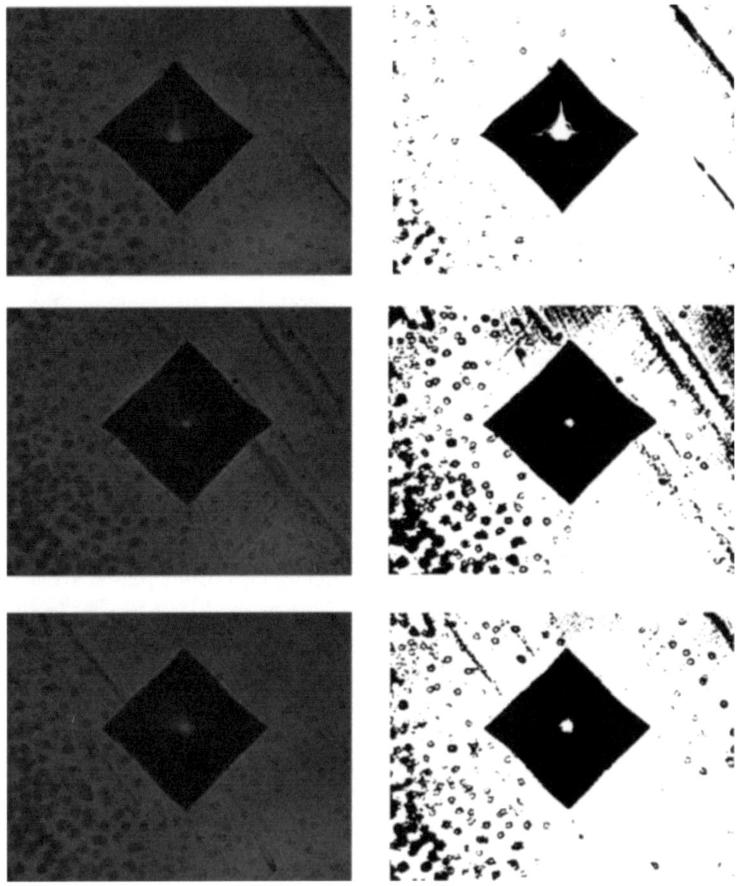

Figure 2.
Indentation images and their binary images.

3. Morphological filtering

For the binary image G, any set A of black pixels, and a (small) pixel set S called structuring element, the *dilatation* of A by S is the set $A \oplus S$ of all pixels $p = \left(p_x, p_y\right)$ such that $x_1 \leq p_x \leq x_{\max}, y_1 \leq p_y \leq y_{\max}$, and $p = a + s = \left(a_x + s_x, a_y + s_y\right)$ for some $a = \left(a_x, a_y\right) \in A$, $s = \left(s_x, s_y\right) \in S$ [27]. Thus, the dilation consists of extending the set of black points in G converting into black all pixels of $A \oplus S$. The *erosion* of A by S is the pixel set $A \ominus S = \{p \in A : p + s \in A \forall s \in S\}$. Erosion reduces the set of black points in G converting into White all pixels of A which do not belong to $A \ominus S$. Erosion followed by dilation is called morphological opening, whereas morphiological closing is defined as Erosion of a dilated set.

The filters applied to the binarization techniques reported in [27, 28] consists in morphological opening of the set of black pixels in G, by a structuring element distinct from those used in works previously published. Based on the a- priori knowledge that the indentation region has a rhombic shape. Moreover, these binarization techniques use a structuring element S of diamond shape of 10 pixels radius. This morphological opening sustantively reduces structural noise of the image, making possible to find the interest object (indentation region) as the largest connected region of black pixels in the next step. In addition, it preserves size and shape of the indentation. Finally, through region growing, which is a standard procedure in image processing the image segmentation is completed. In a binary image, region growing consists in determining all connected components of black pixels, where the algorithms reported in [27, 28] applies 8-connectivity.

Figure 3 shows images together with their binary versions, and the results of morphological filtering. The first example contains a slightly deformed indentation and the second presents surface imperfections. Nevertheless, many of these types of images present some shading by lots of lighting and additionally, a light sopt in the image center, both problems caused by the light reflection capacity when capturing the image through a camera. Thus, the algortihm semi-automatic reported in [27] is

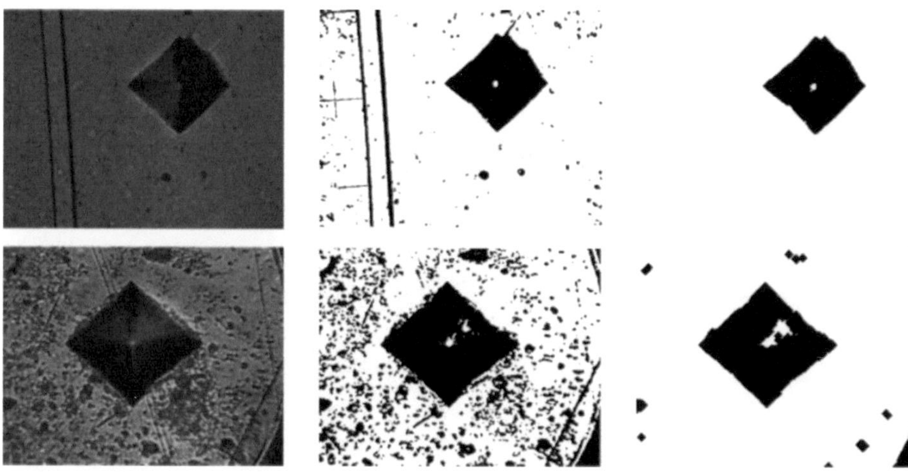

Figure 3.
Indentation images (first column), binary versions (second column) and morphological filtering (third column).

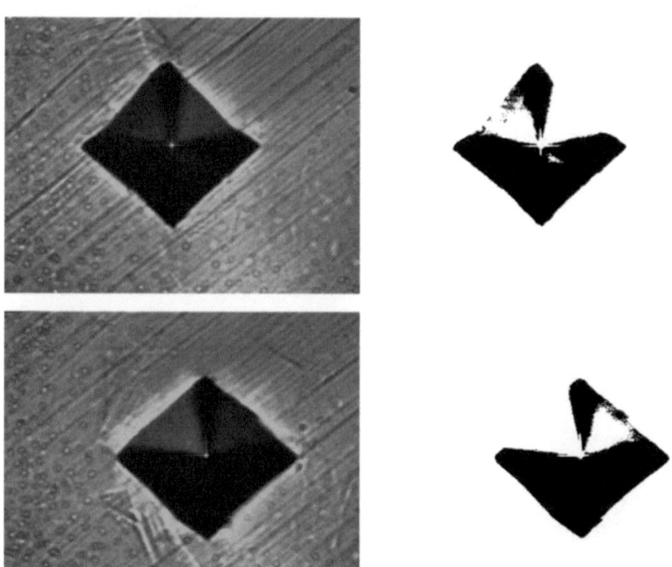

Figure 4.
Indentation images with low contrast, where the algorithm reported in [27] fails in binarization technique.

not suitable for indentation images with low contrast in relation to the adjacent image, as show in the **Figure 4**.

4. Image segmentation automatically evaluating maximum and average gray values like binarization criteria

The algorithm reported in [28] uses image segmentation via binarization, automatically evaluating the mean and extreme gray values by means of standard histogram equalization so as to determine the optimal binarization threshold from each input image. The binarization of the input image use the average gray value, a standard histogram applied to the input image, and the difference to the maximum gray values to determine the threshold values (τ) for binarization. The highest frquency of occurence $f_h = \max h(i)$ (where $h(i)$ is the histogram of the image with a number i of gray values), average f_{mean}, and maximum $f_{\max}$ gray values are global characteristics determined by the input image F . Unlike semi-automatic binarization reported in [27], the image segmentation reported in [28] evaluate maximum and average gray values under the following binarization criterion:

$$\left| f(x,y) - f_{\max} \right| > \tau \tag{1}$$

The binarization using (1) with $\tau = \tau_0 = f_{mean}$ is applied to indentation images with gray levels distribuided along the dynamic range of $h(i)$ as shown in **Figure 5**, where $f_{mean} \cong f_h$ and f_{mean} are located to approximately half of the dynamic range $h(i)$.

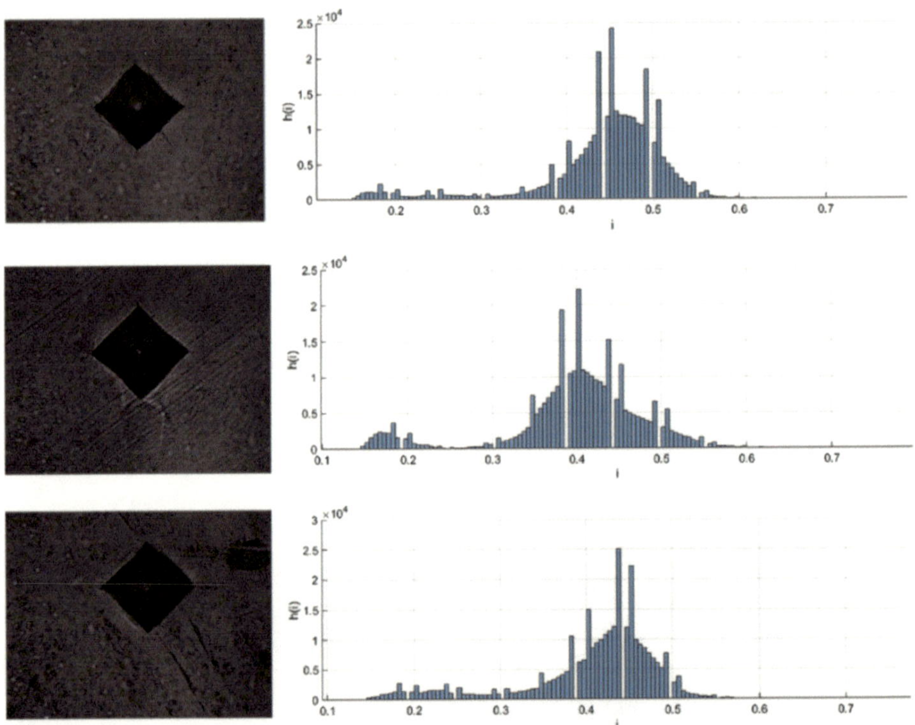

Figure 5.
Indentation images where $f_{mean} \cong f_h$ and f_{mean} are located to approximately half of the dynamic range $h(i)$.

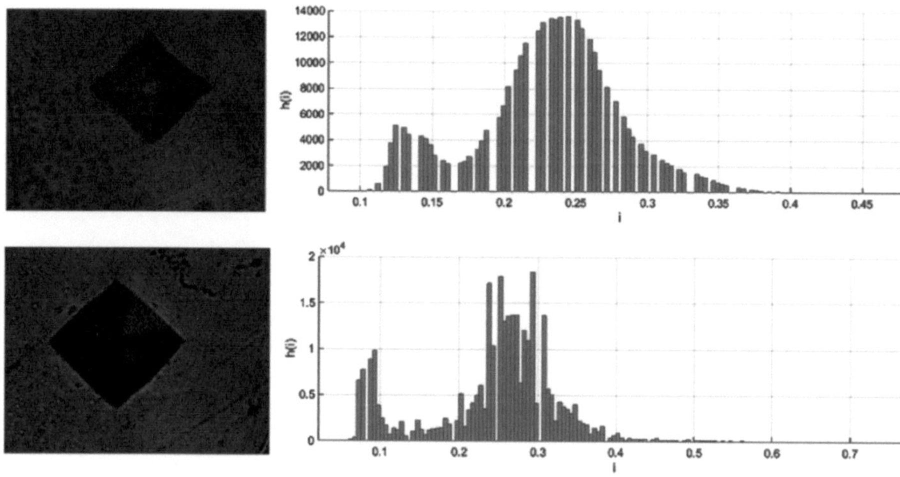

Figure 6.
Dark-field images of indentation and their $h(i)$.

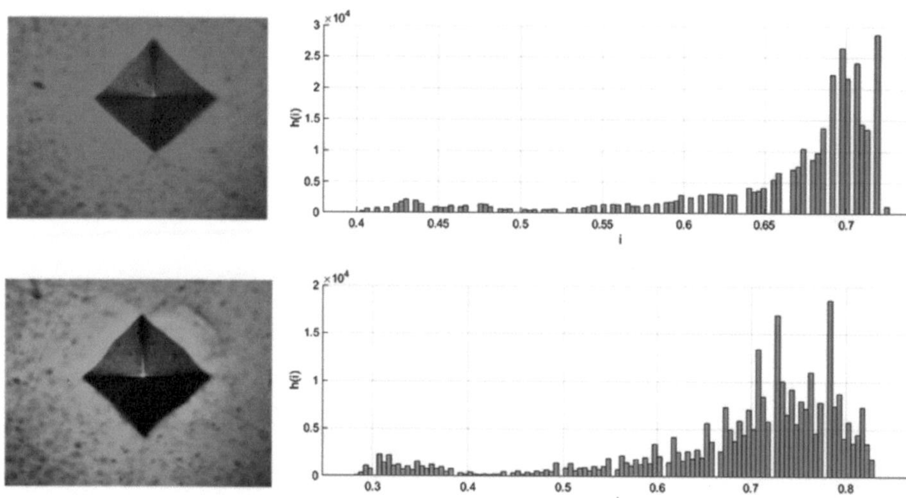

Figure 7.
Indentation images with light gray levels and their $h(i)$.

The highest frequency of occurrence on the left of the dynamic range is presented in dark-field images of indentation, as shown in **Figure 6**. For these images in $\tau = \tau_0 = f_{mean}$ prevents good binarization. Thus, Eq. (1) is evaluated for $\tau = \tau_0 + |(f_h - f_{mean})|$ until good binarization can be obtained.

To indentation images with light gray levels present histogram with a landslide of gray values, where the highest frequency of ocurrence falls to the right of the dynamic range $h(i)$, as shown in **Figure 7**. In these images, Eq. (1) is evaluated for $\tau = \tau_0 - |(f_h - f_{mean})|$ until better image segmentation is achieved and some feature of the object of interes may be obtained, for example the indentation vertices [28].

Thus, the binarization reported in [28] can be resumed as shown in the flow chart of the **Figure 8**.

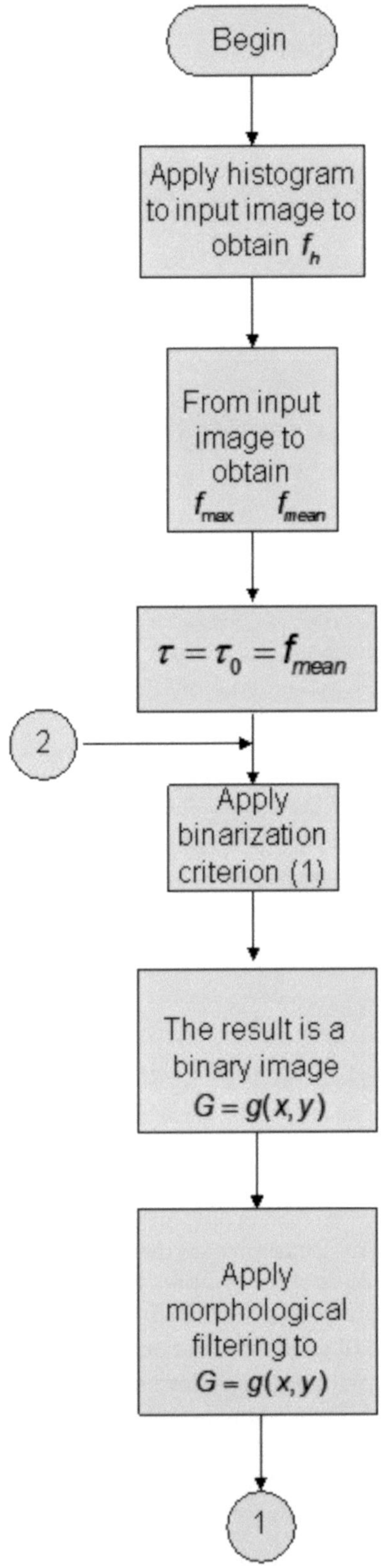
Begin
Apply histogram to input image to obtain f_h
From input image to obtain f_{max} f_{mean}
$\tau = \tau_0 = f_{mean}$
2
Apply binarization criterion (1)
The result is a binary image $G = g(x, y)$
Apply morphological filtering to $G = g(x, y)$
1

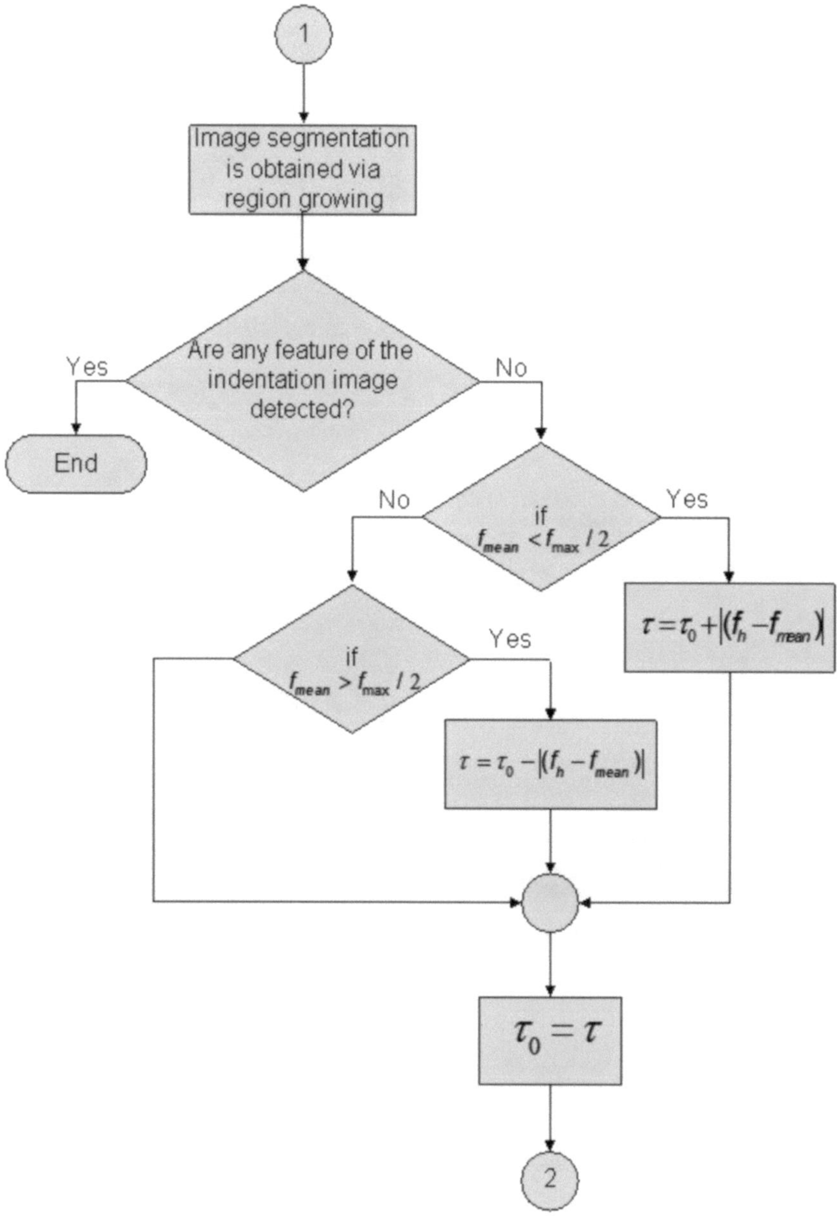

Figure 8.
Image segmentation automatically evaluating maximum and average gray values like binarization criteria.

Figure 9 shows an example of improved binarization in dark-field of indentations applying the algorithm reported in [28]. **Figure 10** shows an example of the algorithm reported in [28] applied in Indentation images with light gray levels.

5. Examples of the techniques

The indentations image are generated through Microdurometers, which use a diamond tip to generate the indentation images. Example, the microdurometer

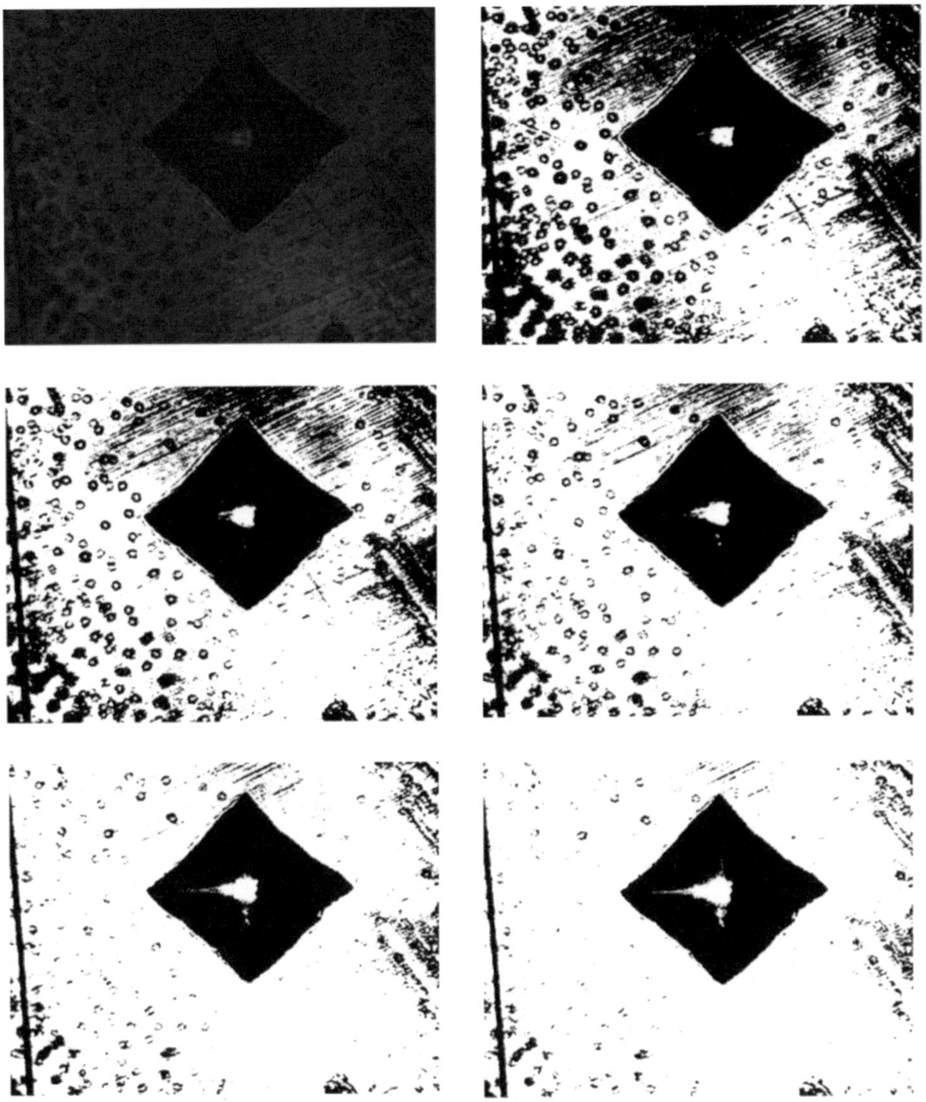

Figure 9.
Example of improved binarization in dark-field of indentation images.

Mitutoyo model HM-125 (see **Figure 11**) use a microscope with up to 100-fold magnification, which it analog video signal was converted to a digital video signal [32], so that it can be stored as 2D indentation images in gray-scale BMP format.

In many indantion images obtained of samples of steel-316 with roughly polished surface, it is enough to apply the semi-automatic segmentation technique to obtain a good binarization of the image. In **Figure 2**, with the values of f_{mean} and $f_{\max}$ are enough to evaluate $|f(x,y) - f_{\max}| > f_{mean}$ and obtain a good binarization (see **Figure 2**). Furthermore, with morphological filter and region growing, reduces structural noise of the image, making possible to find the indentation and other characteristics of the interes object like the indentation vertices applying techniques reported in [27, 28]. Images acquired from samples of steel-316, but with specular-polished surface, present a light spot in the indentation center, generated by the microscope's integrated light source, which these indentation images have low

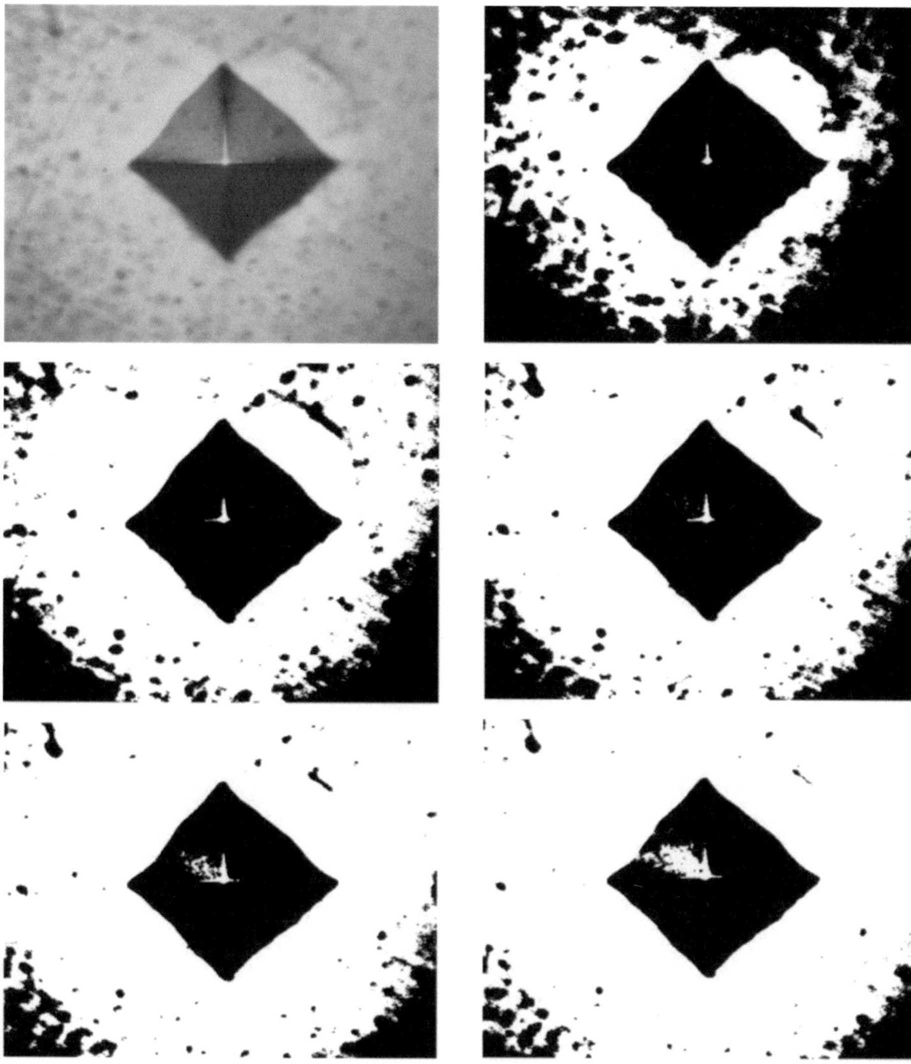

Figure 10.
Example of improved binarization in indentation images with light gray levels.

contrast in relation to the adjacent image area. For these images, the binarization is bad obtained by the semi-automatic segmentation technique, because present a maximum area 8-component such that not coincide with the indentation, as shown in the first image of the **Figure 12**. In addition, samples of steel-316 with roughly polished surface, present dark-field images of indentation, where the morphological filter is insufficient to eliminate pixels detected as false positives for the indentation region, as shown in the second image of the same **Figure 12**.

Thus, images with low contrast have been treated by automatic image segmentation, obtaining a better binarization than the semi-automatic segmentation technique. **Figure 13** shows the improvement of binarization applying the automatic image segmentation technique to the same images in **Figure 12**, which, is observed that in the binarization obtained by the automatic image segmentation the maximum area 8-component coincides with the indentation footprint. In addition, applying techniques reported in [27, 28] the indentation vertices are obtained

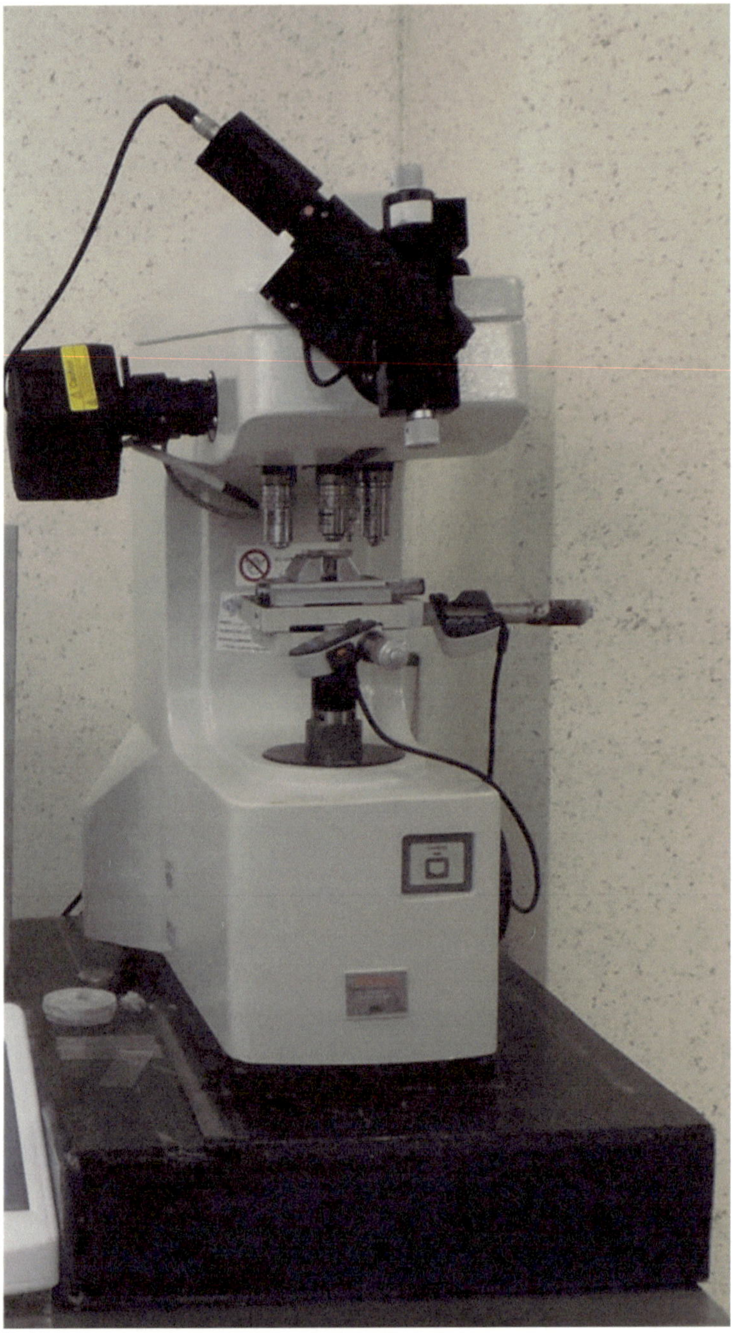

Figure 11.
Microdurometer Mitutoyo HM-125.

satisfactoraly after applying morphological filter and region growing to the final binarization obtained.

The first input image of **Figure 13** satisfies the condition $f_{mean} > \frac{f_{\max}}{2}$ of the automatic segmentation technique, while the second input image satisfies that $f_{mean} < \frac{f_{\max}}{2}$ to obtain the optimal binarization threshold from the second image of **Figure 13**.

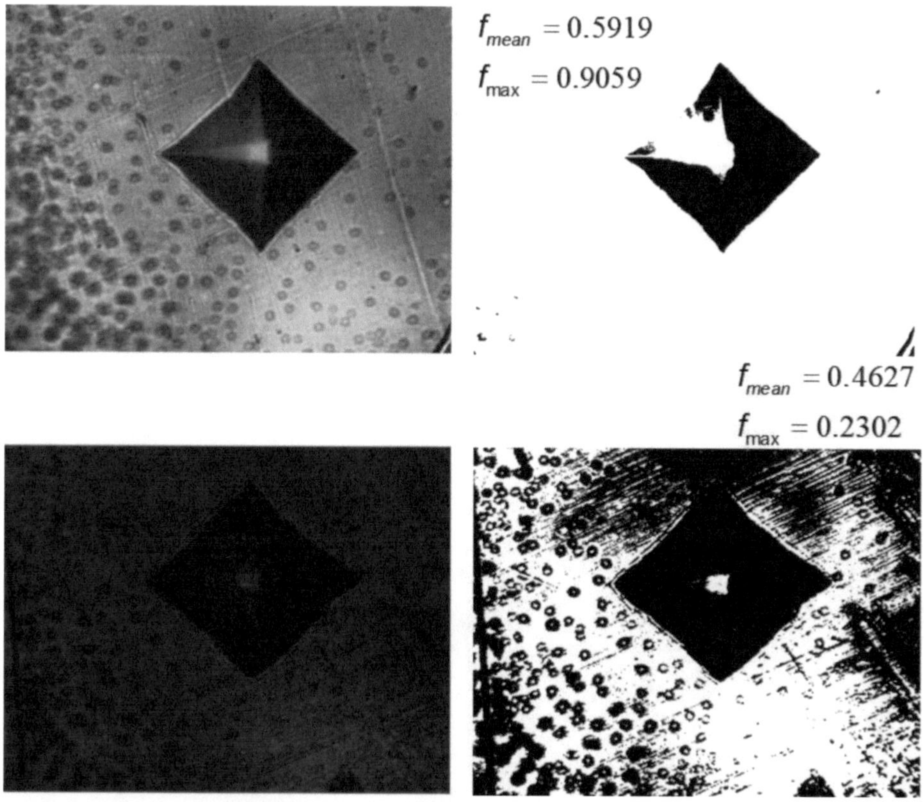

Figure 12.
Indentations images with low contrast (left column). Bad binarization obtained by the semi-automatic segmentation technique (second column).

6. Conclusions

A couple of algorithms were presented in this chapter, which consist in a very simple binarization, based in the average gray value of the input image as threshold and the difference to the maximum gray value as binarization criteria, which presents robustness against image noise and surface imperfections.

A second algorithm presented in this chapter, employed the same binarization criteria for each input image as the firts algorithm. However, the second altering the mean gray values via automatic analysis with standard histogram equalization to determine the optimal binarization threshold. Morphological filtering was applied to the binarized image, followed by a segmentation on the growing region. Therefore, the result obtained is a maximum area black 8-component of the image segmentation by both algorithms. Nevertheless, the second algorithm, unlike the first, evaluates a wide range of indentation images, which the indentation edges are not exactly straight lines, and indentation images with very low contrast relation to the adjacent image area, and where the indentation image presents some shading, thereby resolving illumination problems in the image.

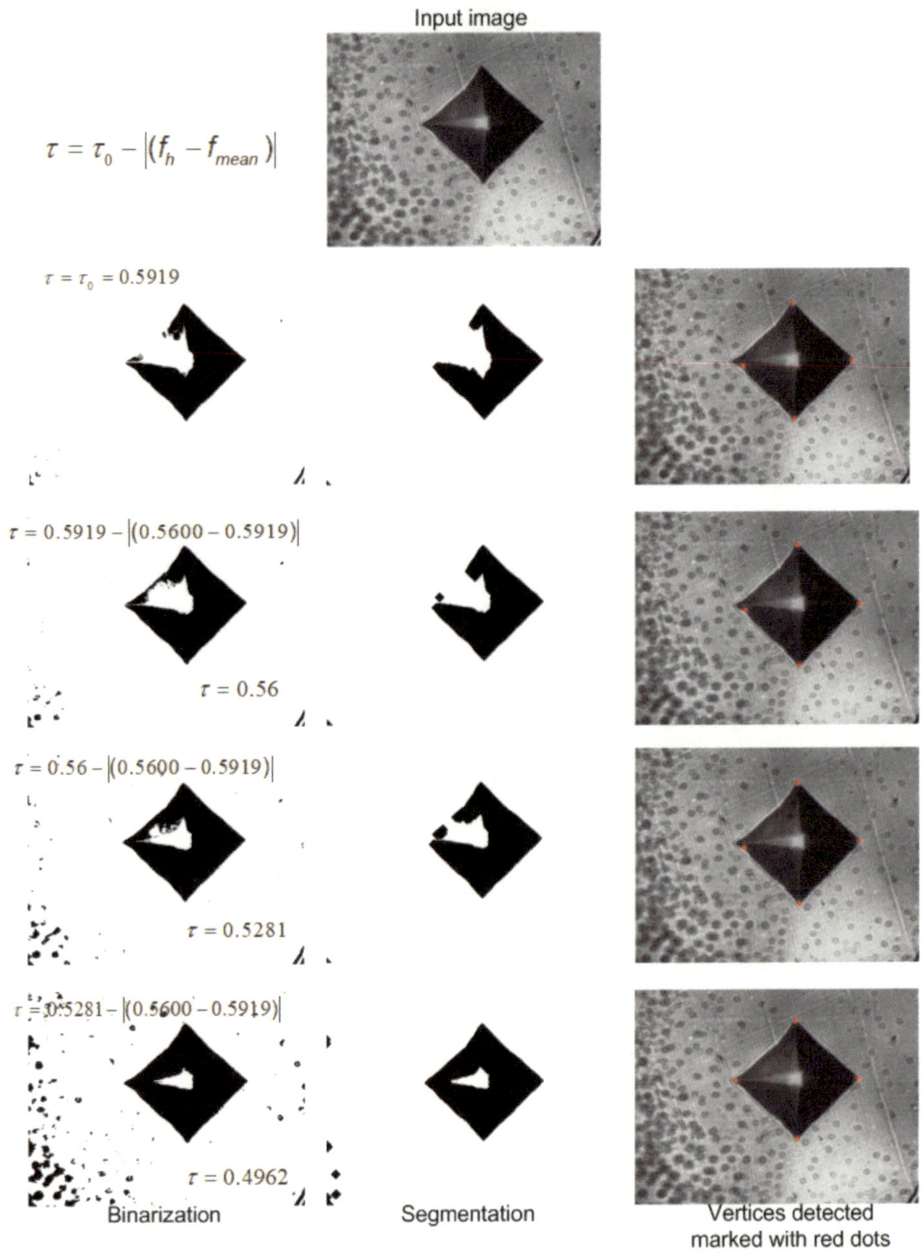
Input image
$\tau = \tau_0 - |(f_h - f_{mean})|$
$\tau = \tau_0 = 0.5919$
$\tau = 0.5919 - |(0.5600 - 0.5919)|$
$\tau = 0.56$
$\tau = 0.56 - |(0.5600 - 0.5919)|$
$\tau = 0.5281$
$\tau = 0.5281 - |(0.5600 - 0.5919)|$
$\tau = 0.4962$
Binarization
Segmentation
Vertices detected marked with red dots

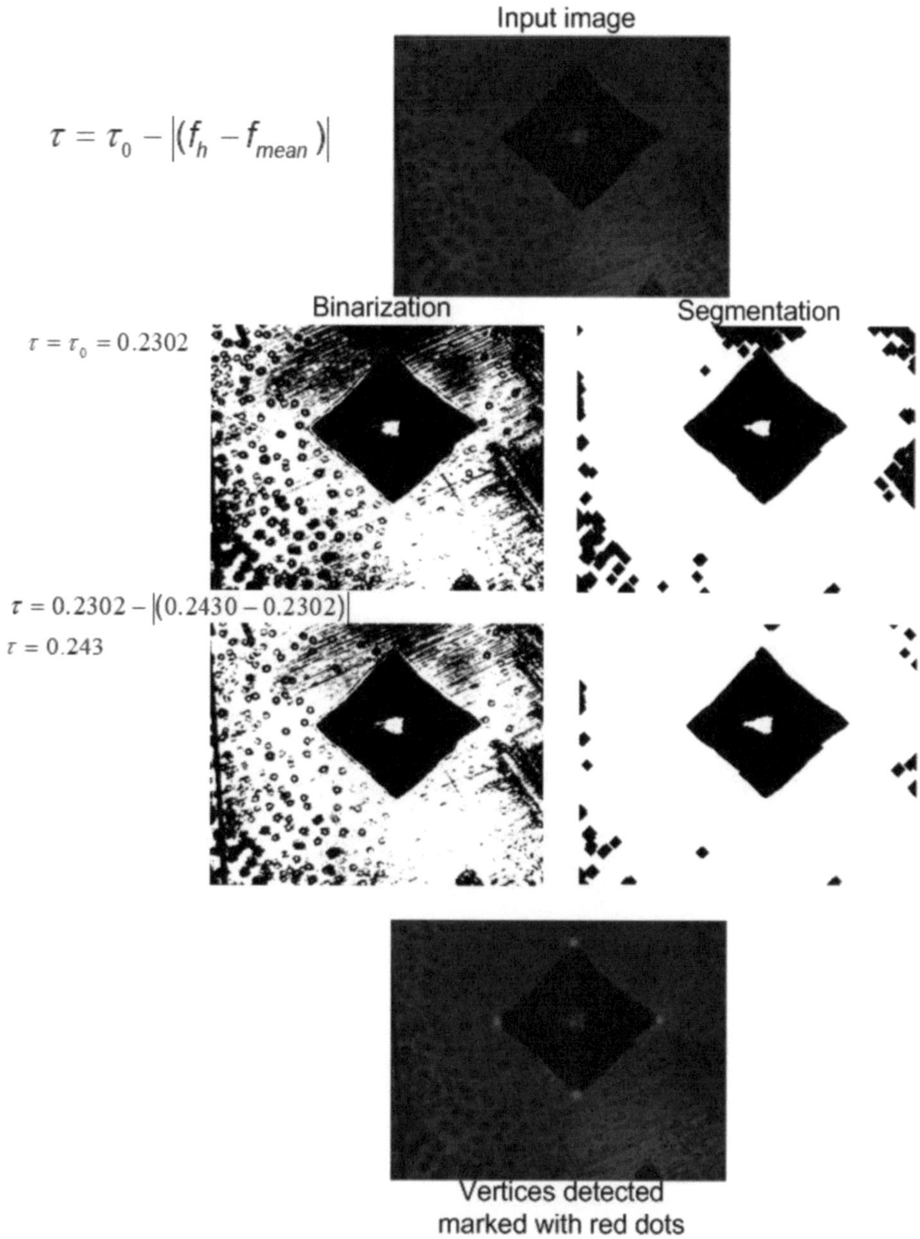

Figure 13.
Sequence to obtain good binarization through the automatic segmentation technique applied to indentations images with low contrast.

Author details

Saúl Manuel Domínguez Nicolás
Micro and Nanotechnology Research Center, Universidad Veracruzana, Boca del Río, Veracruz, Mexico

*Address all correspondence to: saudominguez@uv.mx

References

[1] Otsu N. (1979) A Threshold selection method from Gray-level Histograms. IEEE Trans. Sys., Man., Cyber. 9, 1, pp 62-66.

[2] Canny J. (1986) A Computational Approach to Edge Detection. IEEE Trans. Pattern Analysis and Machine Intelligence. 9, 6, pp. 679-698, https://doi.org/10.1109/TPAMI.1986.4767851

[3] Davis LS. (1975) A Survey of Edge Detection Techniques. Computer Graphics and Image processing. 4, 3, pp. 248-270, https://doi.org/10.1016/0146-664X(75)90012-X

[4] Andreão RV, Boudy J. (2007) Combining Wavelet Transform and Hidden Markov Models for ECG Segmentation. EURASIP Journal on Applied Signal Processing. 1, pp. 1-8 https://doi.org/10.1155/2007/56215

[5] Qin XJ, Jiang JH. (2007) Canny Operator Based Level Set Segmentation Algorithm for Medical Images. *Proceedings of the 1st International Conference on Bioinformatics and Biomedical Engineering.* (Wuhan, China). https://doi.org/10.1109/ICBBE.2007.232

[6] Beucher S, Meyer F. (1990) Morphological segmentation. Journal of Visual Communication and Image Representation. 1, 1, pp. 21-46. https://doi.org/10.1016/1047-3203(90)90014-M

[7] Adams R, Bischof L. (1994) Seeded Region Growing. IEEE Trans. on Pattern Analysis and Machine Intelligence. 6, 6, pp. 641-647. https://doi.org/10.1109/34.295913

[8] Phole R, Toennies KD. (2001) Segmentation of Medical Images Using Adaptive Region Growing. *Proceedings of he SPIE Medical Imaging.* (San Diego, California, USA). 4322. https://doi.org/10.1117/12.431013

[9] Yi J, Ra JB (2001). Vascular Segmentation Algorithm Using Locally Adaptive Region Growing Based on Centerline Estimation. *Proceedings of he SPIE Medical Imaging.* (San Diego, California, USA). 4322. https://doi.org/10.1117/12.431012

[10] Pan ZG, Lu JF (2007). A Bayes-Based Region-Growing Algorithm for Medical Image Segmentation. Computing in Science & Engineering. 9, 4, pp. 32-38. https://doi.org/10.1109/MCSE.2007.67

[11] Grau V, Mewes AUJ. (2004). Improved Watershed Transform for Medical Image Segmentation Using Prior Information. IEEE Transactions on Medical Imaging. 23, 4, pp. 447-458. https://doi.org/10.1109/TMI.2004.824224

[12] Ng HP, Ong SH, Foong KWC, Goh PS, Nowinski WL. (2006). Medical Image Segmentation Using K-Means Clustering and Improved Watershed Algorithm. *Proceedings of the IEEE Southeast Symposium on Image Analysis and Interpretation.* (Denver, Colorado, USA). https://doi.org/10.1109/SSIAI.2006.1633722

[13] Hamarneh G, Li X. (2009). Watershed Segmentation Using Prior Shape and Appearance Knowledge. Image and Vision Computing. 27, 1, pp. 59-68. https://doi.org/10.1016/j.imavis.2006.10.009

[14] Sugimoto T, Kawaguchi T (1997) Development of an automatic Vickers hardness testing system using image processing technology. *IEEE Trans.* Ind. Electron. 44. 696-702. https://doi.org/10.1109/41.633474

[15] Ji Y, Xu A (2009) A new method for automatically measurement of Vickers hardness using thick line hough transform and least square method. *2nd Inter. Cong. Image Sign. Proc.*, Tianjin,

China. https://doi.org/10.1109/CISP.2009.5305653

[16] Kang S, Kim J, Park C, Kim H, Kwon D (2010) Conventional Vickers and true instrumented indentation hardness determined by instrumented indentation tests. J. Mater. Res. 25 337-343. https://doi.org/10.1557/JMR.2010.0045

[17] Filho P, Cavalcante T, de Alburquerque V, Tavares J (2010) Brinell and Vickers hardness measurement using image processing and analysis techniques. J. Test. Eval. 38 88-94. https://doi.org/10.1520/JTE102220

[18] Barati F, Latifi M, Moayeri far E, Mosallanejad MH, Saboori A (2019) Novel AM60-SiO_2 nanocomposite produced via ultrasound-assisted casting; production and characterization *Materials* **12** 3976. https://doi.org/10.3390/ma12233976

[19] Momber AW, Irmer M, Marquardt T (2020) Effects of polymer hardness on the abrasive wear resistance of thick organic offshore coatings *Prog.* Org. Coat. 146 105720. https://doi.org/10.1016/j.porgcoat.2020.105720

[20] Li M, Wang S, Wang Q, Zhao Z, Duan C, Zhao D, Zhang L, Wang Y (2020) Microstructure and mechanical propertis of MoAlB particles reinforced Al matrix composites by interface modification with in situ formed $Al_{12}Mo$ *J. Alloys Compd.* **823** 153813. https://doi.org/10.1016/j.jallcom.2020.153813

[21] Almonani MA, Hayajneh MT, Al-Shrida M INvestigation of mechanical and tribological properties of hybrid green eggshells and graphite-reinforced aluminum composites *J. Braz. Soc. Mech. Sci. Eng.* **42** 45. https://doi.org/10.1007/s40430-019-2130-z

[22] Wang C, Song L, Xie Y (2020) Mechanical and electrical characteristics of WB_2 synthesized at high pressure and high temperature *Materials* **13** 1212. https://doi.org/10.3390/ma13051212

[23] Gadermayr M, Maier A, Uhl A (2012) The impact of unfocused Vickers indentation images on segmentation performance. In: Bebis G et al. (eds) Advances in Visual Computing. *ISVC 2012 Lect Notes Comp. Sci.* 7432 Spinger, Berlín, Heidelberg. https://doi.org/10.1007/978-3-642-33191-6_46

[24] Gadermayr M, Maier A, Uhl, A (2011) Algorithms for microindentation measurement in automated Vickers hardness testing. *Proc. SPIE 8000 10th Int. Conf. Qual. Control Artif. Vis.* 80000M. https://doi.org/10.1117/12.890894

[25] Gadermayr M and Uhl A (2012) Dual – resolution active contours segmentation of Vickers indentation images with shape prior initialization In: Elmoataz A, Mammass D, Lezoray O, Nouboud F and Aboutajdine D (eds) *Image Signal Processing* (ICISP 2012) *Lect. Notes Comp. Sci*. 7340 362-369 Springer, Berlin, Heidelberg. https://doi.org/10.1007/978-3-642-31254-0_41

[26] Papari G and Petkov N (2011) Edge and line oriented contour detection: State of the art. *Image Vis.* Comput. **29** 79-103. https://doi.org/10.1016/j.imavis.2010.08.009

[27] Domínguez-Nicolás SM, Wiederhold P (2018) Indentation image analysis for Vickers hardness testing. *15th Int. Conf. Elect. Eng. Comput. Sci. Autom. Contr.* (*CCE*). México. https://doi.org/10.1109/ICEEE.2018.8533881

[28] Domínguez-Nicolás SM, Herrera – May AL, García-González L, Zamora-peredo L, Hernández-Torres J, Martínez-Castillo J, Morales-González EA, Cerón-Álvarez CA, Escobar-Pérez A. (2021). Algorithm for automatic detection and measurement of Vickers indentation hardness using image processing. *Measurement Science*

and Technology. 32, pp. 1-14. https://doi.org/10.1088/13561-6501/abaa66

[29] Gademayr M, Maier A, Uhl A (2012) Robust algorithm for automated microindentation measurement in Vickers hardness testing. J. Electron. Imag. 21 021109. https://doi.org/10.1117/1.JEI.21.2.021109

[30] Maier A, Uhl A (2012) The AreaMap operator and its application to Vickers hardness testing images. Intern. J. Fut. Gener. Commun. Netw. 5 123967509.

[31] Maier A, Uhl A (2013) Areamap and Gabor filter based Vickers hardness indentation measurement. *21st Eur. Sign. Proc. Conf. (EUSIPCO),* Marrakech, Morocco, 1-5.

[32] Domínguez-Nicolás SM, Argüelles-Lucho P, Wiederhold P (2016) FPGA based image acquisition and graphic interface for hardness tests by indentation. Int. J. Adv. Comput. Technol. 5 6-16.

Chapter 3

Object Recognition and Tracking Using the Particle Estimator

Edgardo Comas and Adrián Stácul

Abstract

In this chapter we describe the particle estimators and its effectiveness for tracking objects in video sequences. The particles estimators are specifically advantageous in transition state models and measurements, especially when these are non-linear and not Gaussian. Once the target object to follow has been identified (in position and size) its main characteristics are obtained using algorithms such as FAST, SURF, BRIEF or ORB. As the particle estimator is a recursive Bayesian estimator, where observations update the probability of validating a hypothesis, that is, they use all the available information to reduce the amount of uncertainty present in an inference or decision problem. Therefore, the main characteristics of the object to follow are those that will determine the probability of validating the hypothesis in the particle estimator. Finally, as an example, the application of a particle estimator is described in a real case of tracking an object in a sequence of infrared images.

Keywords: recognition, tracking, estimator, image analysis, image processing

1. Introduction

The first step in tracking object in an image sequence is to identify the reference object to be tracked; this will allow determining its attributes to carry out its identification by means of some of the main characteristics of the image of the object, such as the characteristics points. It should be noted that if is known: the initial position of the object to be tracked in the camera coordinates and the mathematical model of the camera, it is possible, in addition to tracking the object, to estimate its coordinates and moving in this reference system. One of the techniques applied for object tracking to which we will particularly refer is the particle estimator. This technique is a special type of Monte Carlo sequential method, one of its main advantages being its applicability to any model of transition of states and observations, especially when these are non-linear and non-Gaussian [1]. Although the Kalman estimator, which is applied to systems where the system evolution and measurement models are linear, with Gaussian noise, and with known mean and variance; has extensions to nonlinear models by applying techniques to achieve linearity, the Gaussian additive noise constraint cannot be overcome [1, 2].

Therefore, the particle estimators do not have the restrictive hypothesis of the Kalman estimator, so they can be applied to non-linear models with non-Gaussian and multimodal noise, where the reliable numerical estimate is a function of an adequate number of samples [3].

This estimator distributes N particles over the image, and the observations made on each one of them update their probability of validating a hypothesis, that is, they use all the available information to reduce the uncertainty present in an inference or decision problem [2]. In some cases where the images are not clear or noisy, particularly those acquired through infrared cameras, it is necessary to make an improvement before applying the estimator; generally this improvement is based on a reduction in the incidence of the background image, for the special case of infrared images subtracting the value from the mean intensity and modifying its histogram to increase the contrast result a good choice.

Faced with rapid and unpredictable movements of the referent or the camera, the resampling process considers a scattering value based on the number of valid particles, so that the area covered during tracking is dynamically modified. Basically, the particle estimator provides us with a framework, in which it is possible to insert different algorithms for the recognition of the reference image in each particle; some of them are SURF, BRIEF, ORB, etc. These algorithms have the ability to generate a set of invariant features against some image variations, such as: scaling, rotation, illumination and with robustness against occlusion conditions.

2. Particle estimator tracking

To define the state estimation problem let us consider the system model, composed of the state evolution and observation models described by the following equations:

$$X_k = f(X_{k-1}, v_{k-1}), \tag{1}$$

$$Z_k = h(X_k, n_k). \tag{2}$$

Where $X \in R^n$ contains all the state variables that will be dynamically estimated, f is the non-linear function of the state variables, $v \in R^n$ represents the state noise system, $Z \in R^n$ are all observations related with the state variables by (Eq. (2)), $n \in R^n$ is the measurement noise, and h is known as an observation model. Remembering that $P(a|b)$ is the conditional probability of a if b, then the evolution and observation models given by (Eqs. (1) and (2)) are based on the following hypotheses referring to the following sequences [2, 4]:

a. $X_k, k = 1, 2, \ldots$ is a Markov process

$$P(X_k|X_0, X_1, \ldots X_{k-1}) = P(X_k|X_{k-1}), \tag{3}$$

b. $Z_k, k = 1, 2, \ldots$ is a Markov process regarding the historical data of X such that

$$P(Z_k|X_0, X_1, \ldots X_k) = P(Z_k|X_k), \tag{4}$$

c. and the sequence of past observations only depends on its history, that is

$$P(X_k|X_{k-1}, Z_{k-1}) = P(X_k|X_{k-1}). \tag{5}$$

Considering that the system and observation noises $v_i \wedge v_j$ and $n_i \wedge n_j$ are mutually independent of $i \wedge j$ and also the initial state for all $i \neq j$; and on the other hand we know that $P(X_0|Z_0) = P(X_0)$, then, the two-step Bayesian estimator, prediction and update allows us to obtain the probability density $P(X_i|Z_i) = P(X_i)$ [3, 5].

The particle estimator represents the posterior probability density of a random set of samples with their probabilities of validation with the hypothesis, so it is possible to estimate the most likely particle from this set. When we make the number of particles approaches to infinity this process approaches to the a posteriori likelihood function, and the solution approaches an optimal Bayesian estimator [5].

To go into the details of the particle estimator for object tracking, we will rely on the importance sampling method, taking a set of samples from the state space, which characterizes the a posteriori probability density function $p(X_{0:k}|Z_{1:k})$ for the state:

$$X^i_{0:k} = \{X_i, i = 0, \dots, k\}, \tag{6}$$

while that the corresponding observations are $Z_{0:k} = \{Z_i, i = 0, \dots k\}$, then, the a posteriori density in t_k can be approximated by:

$$p(X_{0:k}|Z_{1:k}) \approx \sum_{i=1}^{N} W^i_k \delta\left(X_{0:k} - X^i_{0:k}\right), \tag{7}$$

where $\delta(.)$ is Dirac's delta function, N the total number of particles and $\{W^i_k\}_{i=1}^{N}$ are the assigned weighting.

Considering the hypotheses corresponding to the expressions (Eqs. (1) and (2)) the density a posteriori (Eq. (7)) can be written as [6, 7]:

$$p(X_k|Z_{1:k}) \approx \sum_{i=1}^{N} W^i_k \delta\left(X_k - X^i_k\right), \tag{8}$$

and the evaluation of the weights within the importance sampling principle assumes that there is an evaluable probability density function $p_{(X)}$ such that:

$$W^i_k \alpha p(X_k|Z_{1:k}) \tag{9}$$

and W^i_k are normalized according to (Eqs. (10) and (11)).

$$\sum_{i=1}^{N} W^i_k = 1, \therefore \tag{10}$$

$$W^i_k = \frac{w_k\left(X^i_{i=1:n}\right)}{\sum_{j=1}^{N} w_k\left(X^j_{j=1:n}\right)} \tag{11}$$

This algorithm has a common problem known as the degeneracy phenomenon, which manifests itself after a few states, where all but a few particles (usually one) have negligible weight [3, 6]. This can be solved resampling the particles, however this creates another problem, which is the increasing information uncertainty arising in the random sampling process [8]. However, this problem can be detected by means of what is known as the effective sample size N_{eff}, which can be estimated by means of the (Eq. (12)).

$$N_{eff} = \frac{1}{\sum_{i=1}^{N} \left(W^i_k\right)^2} \tag{12}$$

When all particles have the same weight, i.e. $W_k^i = \frac{1}{N}$, for $= 1, \dots, N$, then the effectiveness is maximum and equal to $N_{eff} = N$, but in the case where all but one particle has zero weight, the effectiveness is minimum and equal to $N_{eff} = 1$ [7].

While the correct choice of the probability density function $p_{(X)}$ to evaluate the particles weights (Eq. (9)), minimizes the problem of the degeneracy phenomenon; but to solve it, a resampling has to be incorporated into the algorithm; this incorporation is known as the Sequential Importance Resampling (SIR). This technique is applied in the case where the effective sample size N_{eff} falls below a threshold value N_T, its effect is to remove particles with small weights and replicate those with greater weights.

2.1 Particle estimator algorithm

In the following, we describe the six steps of the particle estimator algorithm applied to video object tracking:

a. Design:

- An observation function $H_{(k)}$, used for the evaluation of the similarity probability for each particle with the referent object.
- Determine whether image pre-processing is required.
- The number of particles N.
- The threshold number of particles N_{eff}, to determine which type of resampling strategy to use.
- The noise distribution function $\chi_{(k)}$, applied for resampling.

b. Initialization:

- Identification on the image the object to be tracked in its position and size; this operation is performed by the user and defining the reference particle.
- Determination of its main characteristics by means of the observation function $H_{(k)}$; generating the information for the identification of the reference particle.
- Generation of a set of N particles in random position over the whole image, if there is a priori information of its location; this is used for the positioning of the particles centered on it, and over this a random distribution.
- The set of particles are initialized with the normalized weights, with the same values $W_k = \frac{1}{N}$.

c. Update:

- For each particle, their normalized weights are calculated, based on the state probability of similarity to the reference.

- From the particles set, extract a sub set with the particles most likely to match the reference particle.

- With the subset of particles most likely to match the reference particle, the most probable location and size of the object is determined a priori.

d. Resampling:

- The effective number of particles N_{eff} is evaluated, and if it is lower than the threshold value N_T, the lowest weight particles are discarded.

- From this new subset of particles most likely to match the reference particle, the new set of N particles for the next state is created.

- The state of this new set of particles is modified by introducing the additive noise $\chi_{(k)}$, that brings variability to the system.

e. Completion:

- You are returned to the Update stage c), as long as the data sequence is not finished.

2.2 Observation function

Observation functions are those that allow me to extract the main characteristics of an image. In the particle estimator they are used to obtain the main characteristics of the reference image and those of the particles. These sets of main characteristics allow determine the probability of similarity between the reference and each particle. Some of the main algorithms are described below.

2.2.1 Features from accelerated segment test (FAST) algorithm

The FAST algorithm is basically searching over the whole image the points where the changes in intensity in all directions are significantly (corner detection method) [9]. The principal advantage of this algorithm is its high speed performance, and is very suitable for real time applications in computer vision processing. Exist several technics to find a characteristic point in an image; two of this is described below.

In the first one, and as parameters of the algorithm, a threshold value T and a radius r are defined for the evaluation. On the pixel p to evaluate and which has an intensity I_p, a Bresenham circle of radius r is considered (see **Figure 1**).

This circle of radius r defines a set of N points, if in this circle there is a set of n pixels whose inensity is greater than $(I_p + T)$ or less than $(I_p - T)$, then the pixel p can be considered as a characteristic point. The values taken by the authors after the experimental results are: $n \geq 0.75N$ to consider a pixel p as a characteristic point, and the value of the radius $r = 3$, which defines $N = 16$ and $n = 12$.

In a first step, the intensity I_p of pixel p is compared with the intensity of the pixels 1, 5, 9, and 13, if 3 of these 4 pixels meet the threshold criteria, then it is checked if there are at least 12 pixels that meet with this criteria to consider it as a characteristic pixel.

This procedure must be repeated for all pixels in the image and its drawbacks are: for values of $n < 12$ a large number of characteristics points are generated, and

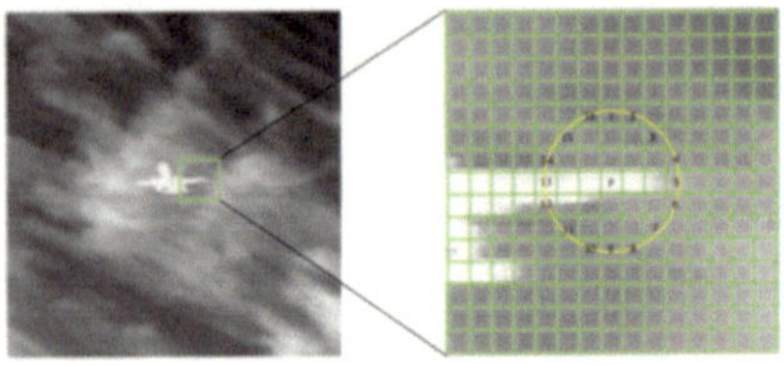

Figure 1.
A Bresenham circle of radius r.

having to evaluate all points of the circle slows down the algorithm. To improve the speed of the algorithm a proposal of the authors is to give it a machine learning approach [10].

In the second one, known as Fast Radial Blob Detector (FRBD), the technique consists of applying the Gaussian Laplacian filter to an image $I_{(x,y)}$, the Laplacian operator, as well as detecting the edges very well also detects the noise very well [11]. Therefore a Gaussian filter must be previously applied to the image to reduce its noise level; a Gaussian kernel of width σ to convolve with the image is represented by the (Eq. (13)) to suppress the noise before using Laplace for edge detection (Eq. (14)), and finally (Eq. (15)) represent the kernel of the Gaussian Laplacian filter to convolve with the image (Eq. (16)).

$$G_{(x,y,\sigma)} = \frac{1}{\sqrt{2\pi\sigma^2}} e^{-\left(\frac{x^2+y^2}{2\sigma^2}\right)} \quad (13)$$

$$L_{(x,y)} = \nabla^2 I_{(x,y)} = \frac{d^2 I_{(x,y)}}{dx^2} + \frac{d^2 I_{(x,y)}}{dy^2} \quad (14)$$

$$LoG_{(x,y)} = \Delta G_{(x,y,\sigma)} = \frac{d^2 G_{(x,y,\sigma)}}{dx^2} + \frac{d^2 G_{(x,y,\sigma)}}{dy^2} \quad (15)$$

$$LoG_{(x,y,\sigma)} = \Delta G_{(x,y,\sigma)} * I_{(x,y)} \quad (16)$$

This kernel $\Delta G_{(x,y,\sigma)}$ showed in **Figure 2**, is a feature detector because it finds regions where the image gradients are changing quickly for example blobs, corners and edges.

This FRBD algorithm goes one step further by using a second-order finite-difference approximation on the filtered image. An approximation to the LoG but which can be computed more rapidly is the Difference of Gaussian (DoG) operator, this approximation using a second-order finite differencing which estimates how the filtered image changes at a given pixel. A circle of radius r is constructed with center in a pixel p, and sampled pixels in eight discrete directions are evaluated, refer to the central pixel (**Figure 3**).

Using the sample points $P_{[0\dots8]}$ compute the average pixel difference around pixel $P_{[0]}$ as,

$$\mathrm{F}(\mathrm{x},\mathrm{y},\mathrm{r}) = \mathrm{abs} \sum_{1=1}^{8} \left(\mathrm{P}_{[0]} - \mathrm{P}_{[i]}\right) \quad (17)$$

The average pixel difference (Eq. (17)) is identical to convolving the original image with the kernel of the **Figure 2**.

The features are extracted maximizing the rate of change of $\mathrm{F}(\mathrm{x},\mathrm{y},\mathrm{r})$ respect to r, calculate as first order differencing,

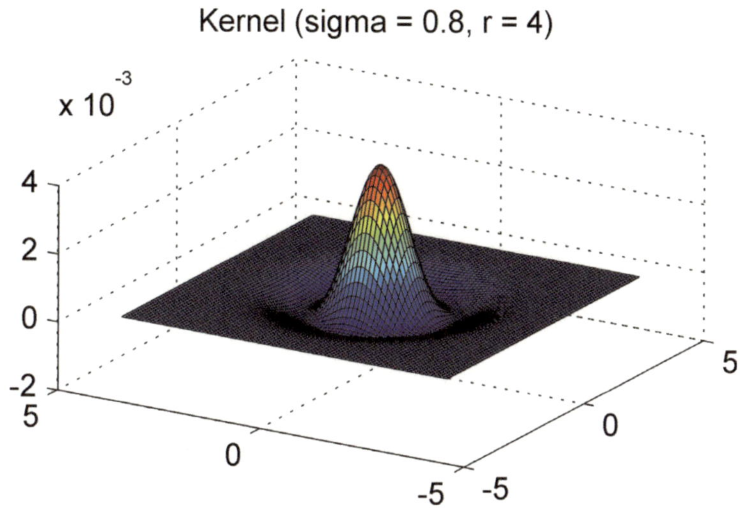

Figure 2.
Kernel of the Gaussian Laplacian filter.

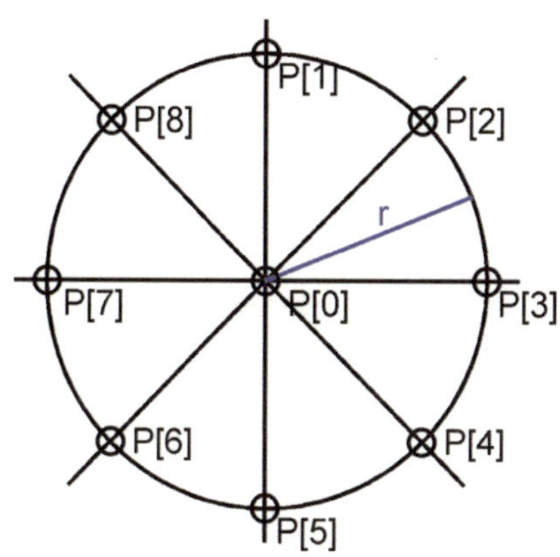

Figure 3.
Eight discrete directions of the sampled pixels.

$$R(x, y, r) = F(x, y, r) - F(x, y, r - 1) \tag{18}$$

if R(x, y, r) is multiplied by the minimum pixel difference,

$$\text{Fmin}(x, y, r) = \min_{i} \left(P_{[0]} - P_{[i]}\right) \tag{19}$$

the pixels that no exhibit changes in intensity in all directions are suppressing.

2.2.2 Speeded-up robust features (SURF) algorithm

The particularity of this algorithm is its ability to determine the characteristics points in an image, which are invariant to changes in: scale, rotations and translations, and partially to illumination changes. This algorithm is an optimization of the Scale Invariant Feature Transform (SIFT) algorithm [12], being its execution speed much higher than the latter [13]. On the other hand, the SURF algorithm produces less information that the SIFT for each characteristic point of the image, although the produced information by the SURF algorithm is more than enough for most applications, including the present one.

The use of integral images in this algorithm makes it very fast to represent at different scales of the original image its differential features. Integral images accelerate the computation at different scales the application of Haar wavelets, and together with the application of the Hessian differential operator allows the determination of key points and their robust descriptor features [2, 11].

Given an image I, and a point $X = (x, y)$ in this image, the Hessian matrix $H_{(X,\sigma)}$ in $X = (x, y)$ to the scale σ is defined as:

$$H_{(X,\sigma)} = \begin{bmatrix} L_{x,x,(X,\sigma)} & L_{y,x,(X,\sigma)} \\ L_{x,y,(X,\sigma)} & L_{y,y,(X,\sigma)} \end{bmatrix}, \tag{20}$$

where $L_{x,x,(X,\sigma)}$, $L_{x,y,(X,\sigma)}$, $L_{y,x,(X,\sigma)}$ and $L_{y,y,(X,\sigma)}$ represent the convolution product of the second derivative of the Gaussian $\frac{\partial^2}{\partial X^2} g_{(X,\sigma)}$ with the Image I in the point $X = (x, y)$ [12], see (Eq. (22)).

$$L_{x,x,(X,\sigma)} = \frac{\partial^2}{\partial X^2} * \left[G_{(x,y,\sigma)} * I_{(x,y)}\right] \tag{21}$$

$$L_{x,x,(X,\sigma)} = \left[\frac{\partial^2}{\partial X^2} * G_{(x,y,\sigma)}\right] * I_{(x,y)} \tag{22}$$

$$\wedge G_{(x,y,\sigma)} = \frac{1}{2\pi\sigma^2} e^{-\frac{x^2+y^2}{2\sigma^2}} \tag{23}$$

The determinant of the Hessian matrix allows the calculation of the scale of the point, defined as follows:

$$\left|H_{(X,\sigma)}\right| = D_{x,x} D_{y,y} - \left(\omega D_{x,y}\right)^2, \tag{24}$$

where $D_{x,x}$, $D_{y,y}$, and $D_{x,y} = D_{y,x}$ are the approximations of the partial derivatives, and ω is the balance factor of the determinant [2], obtained from (Eq. (25)) where $|.|_F$ is the Frobenius norm [3], see (Eq. (26)).

$$w = \frac{\left|L_{x,y,(X,\sigma)}\right|_F \left|D_{y,y}\right|_F}{\left|L_{y,y,(X,\sigma)}\right|_F \left|D_{x,y}\right|_F} \tag{25}$$

$$|A|_F = \sqrt{\sum_{i=1}^{m} \sum_{j=1}^{n} \left(a_{i,j}\right)^2} \tag{26}$$

Applying the Haar-Wavelet filters in a circular area of radius 6*s* provides us a set of outputs in both directions (dx and *dy* respectively), and the mean value of those responses as a dominant direction within the sliding area of $\pi/3$ [12].

Finally the feature descriptors for a certain scale and for each characteristic point are obtained. To do this a rectangular area of $20\sigma \, x \, 20\sigma$ centered on the point is constructed in the dominant orientation. This is divided into four sub-regions of 4*x*4, and for each sub-region the Haar-Wavelet is applied obtaining the horizontal dx and vertical dy responses. A characteristic vector V is formed, and then for each point a total of 64 SURF descriptors are generated [10, 11],

$$V = \left(\sum d_x, \sum d_y, \sum |d_x|, \sum |d_y|\right). \tag{27}$$

2.2.3 Binary robust independent elementary features (BRIEF) algorithm

In terms of execution time, the SURF algorithm performs better than SIFT, but this is not sufficient for current applications for real-time processing of video streams in navigation, augmented reality, etc. To satisfy these applications simpler concepts are applied in algorithms for obtaining fast detectors and descriptors, such as: FAST [14], FASTER [15], CenSurE [16], and SUSurE [17] are some examples of them.

In particular the BRIEF descriptor, like SURF, uses the integral image and applies to a set of very simple binary tests which are adequate to the use of the Hamming distance (distance between two code words, is the number of bit positions in which they differ). This distance is much simpler and faster to evaluate than the Euclidean distance. It is also demonstrated in a practical way that a 32-dimensional BRIEF descriptor achieves similar results to a 64-dimensional SURF descriptor.

This algorithm obtains the descriptors of the characteristics points of the image, and for this a defining a neighboring area centered on this points, this area is known as patch p, which is square and a few pixels high and wide $L\ x\ L$ (see **Figure 4**).

Since, the BRIEF algorithm handles pixel intensity levels this makes it very sensitive to noise, therefore it is necessary to pre-smooth the patch to reduce the sensitivity and increase the accuracy of the descriptors. Is for that, after create a patch centered on the feature point a smooth Gaussian filter is applied to the patch (Eq. (28)),

$$f_{(x,y)} = \frac{1}{2\pi\sigma^2} e^{\left(-\frac{x^2+y^2}{2\sigma^2}\right)}. \tag{28}$$

BRIEF converts the patches into a binary vector representative of it, this descriptor containing only 1 and 0, so each descriptor of a characteristic point is a string of 128–512 bits. After applied the smoothing to the patch p by (Eq. (16)) the patch is converted to binary feature vector as responses of binary test τ, which is define by (Eq. (29)),

$$\tau_{(p;\,x,y)} = \begin{cases} 1 : p_{(x)} < p_{(y)} \\ 0 : p_{(x)} \geq p_{(y)} \end{cases} \tag{29}$$

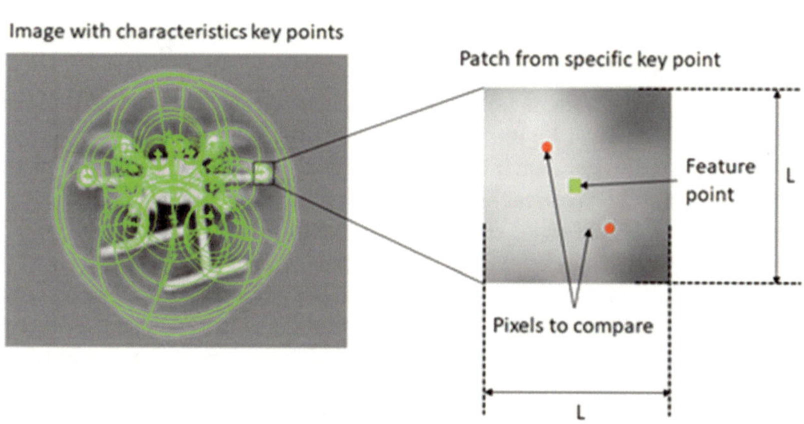

Figure 4.
Patch in an image over a specific key point.

where $p_{(x)}$ is the intensity value of the pixel at point x; then a set of $n(x, y)$ with n equal to 128, 256 or 512, and the location pairs (see **Figure 4**) must be defined as a set of binary tests uniquely. The pixel $p_{(x,y)}$ is located inside the patch, and it is called random pair, for creating a binary feature vector of number *n* is necessary select the random pairs; the most useful functions to this selection are the following five, showed in (Eq. (30)).

$$\left.\begin{array}{ll} I. & (X,Y) \sim \text{Uniform}\left(-\frac{L}{2}, +\frac{L}{2}\right) \\ II. & (X,Y) \sim \text{Gaussian}\left(0, +\frac{1}{25}L^2\right) \\ III. & X \sim \text{Gaussian}\left(0, +\frac{1}{25}L^2\right) \\ & Y \sim \text{Gaussian}\left(x_i, \frac{1}{100}L^2\right) \\ IV. & \text{The } (x_i, y_i) \text{ are randomly sampled} \\ V. & x_i = (0,0)^T \text{ and } y_i \text{ is takes all} \\ & \text{possible values on a coarse polar grid} \end{array}\right\} \tag{30}$$

The advantages characteristics of the BRIEF descriptor are: high-speed processing, little memory usage and strong to illumination and blur change, and disadvantages are: weak to the rotation of the viewpoint, and the change in the position of a light source.

The (Eq. (31)) describes the BRIEF descriptor, but in its application must be in consideration that its matching performance falls sharply with a few degrees in plane rotation.

$$f_{n(p)} = \sum_{i=1}^{n} 2^{i-1}.\tau(p; x_i, y_i) \tag{31}$$

2.2.4 Oriented FAST and rotate BRIEF (ORB) algorithm

The main characteristics of the ORB algorithm compared to its equivalents SIFT and SURF are that the ORB performs the feature detection operations as well as these but with a superior performance; having as an additional advantage that its use is free. It is based on the widely proven FAST and BRIEF algorithms, very good performance and low computational cost.

As the FAST algorithm does not have information about features of orientation and multi-scale, these must be implemented. For the multi-scale response, a scale pyramid is generated, where each level of the pyramid contains a version of the original image but at a lower resolution (**Figure 5**).

Applying to each level (scale) the FAST algorithm (see 2.1.1) we obtain the characteristics points at each level (vertices); as this algorithm also responds to edges, these must be discarded. For this we use the Harris algorithm with a low threshold [18], in order to obtain a large number of characteristic points, which are ordered according to the Harris measure to obtain the desired number of main points.

From there, the orientation is done by means of the intensity centroid [19], which assumes that the intensity of a corner is different from that of its center, and the vector formed between both points is used to calculate its orientation. Rosin defines the moments of a patch by means of (Eq. (32)) as,

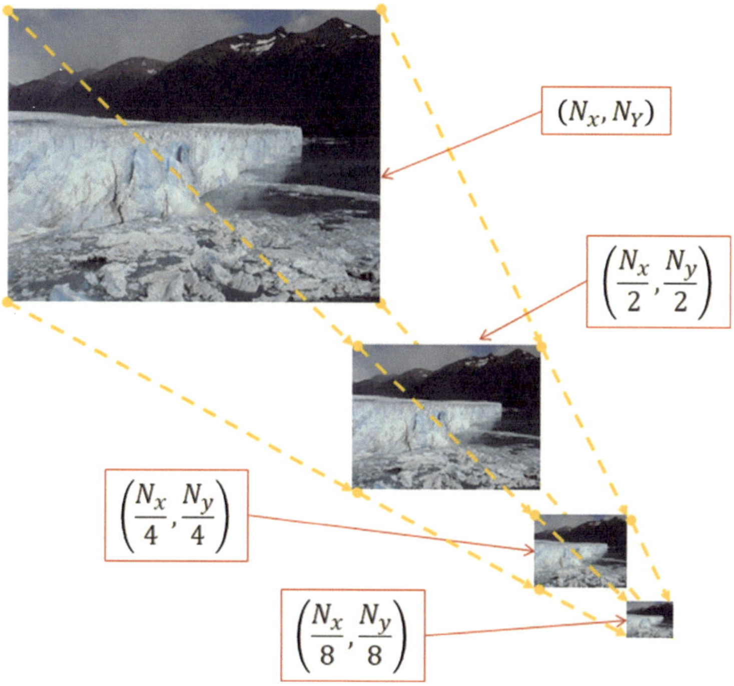

Figure 5.
Multiscale scheme for an image.

$$m_{p,q} = \sum_{x,y} x^p . y^q . I_{(x,y)} \tag{32}$$

and with these moments we can find the centroid by (Eq. (33)),

$$C = \left(\frac{m_{1,0}}{m_{0,0}}, \frac{m_{0,1}}{m_{0,0}}\right). \tag{33}$$

While the orientation of the patch can be calculated by means of the vector $\overrightarrow{OC}$ with origin at the center C of the patch and a point O on its periphery, and is obtained by means of (Eq. (34)),

$$\theta = \text{atan2}(m_{0,1}, m_{1,0}). \tag{34}$$

To improve the invariance of this measurement we must ensure that the calculation of the moments is performed with x and y included in a circular region of radius r contained within the patch.

The table of features for each characteristics point is determined by means of the steered BRIEF method [20], according to the orientation θ of the patch at that point. For each characteristics point (x_i, y_i) we define a 2 x n matrix S (Eq. (35)), and a rotation matrix R_θ as function of the orientation θ of the patch, obtaining an oriented version of the matrix S_θ by (Eq. (36)).

$$S = \begin{bmatrix} x_1 & \cdots & x_n \\ y_1 & \cdots & y_n \end{bmatrix} \tag{35}$$

$$S_\theta = R_\theta S \tag{36}$$

Obtaining the operator steered BRIEF as,

$$g_n(p, \theta) = f_n(p) | (x_i, y_i) \in S_\theta, \tag{37}$$

where $f_n(p)$ is the binary test operator obtained from (Eq. (31)).

To construct the BRIEF pattern search table, the angle θ is discretizing in increments of $2\pi/30$ (12 degrees). All previous tests are ordered by their distance from a mean of 0.5 generating a vector T. Then the first test of T is taken and added to the table of results R, from there the next test of the vector T is taken and compared with all the tests results in R, if its absolute correlation is less than a threshold it is discarded, otherwise it is added to the table of results R, until a total of 256 tests are obtained.

3. Processes in the particle estimator algorithm

Basically this method deploys in the image a series of random particles, possible states of the process in this case the target position and its size; while their weights represent their posteriori probability of the density functions as an estimated from the observations. One of the particularities of the particle estimator is the number of configuration parameters it has, and to optimize its performance, in terms of estimation quality and processing time, they must be properly chosen. Some of these parameters refer to the behavior of the estimator itself and others to the behavior of the SURF algorithm (used here for infrared images), as described below.

For the behavior of the particle estimator:

- Maximum number of particles,
- Probability threshold to consider a particle valid,
- Adaptability in the standard deviation as a function of the number of valid particles for the vector of states in the resampling.

For the behavior of the SURF algorithm:

- Maximum number of characteristics points to be considered,
- Number of scale level, controls the number of filters used per octave,
- The threshold for the determination of the number of blobs to detect,
- Number of octaves, controls the filters and subsample of the image data; larger number of octaves will result in finding larger size blobs.

Then, and for the case of this application (tracking objects in video images) we can describe the processes implemented following the guidelines of the algorithm described in 2.1.

3.1 Initialization

Mainly in this step, the reference particle to follow is selected, and all the parameters described in the previous paragraph are initialized with the design values.

DOI: http://dx.doi.org/10.5772/intechopen.99615

3.2 Particle description

The particle was described by means of a rectangle; and to characterize it we define a state vector for each particle (Eq. (38)).

$$X = \left[x\, y\, w\, h\, \dot{x}\, \dot{y} \dot{w} \dot{h}\right]^T = [p\ v]^T \tag{38}$$

This state vector contains the positions (x, y) and for its size, lengths of width and height (w, h), while for its velocities $(\dot{x}, \dot{y})$ and $\left(\dot{w}\dot{h}\right)$ respectively.

The velocity of the particle is calculated by means of the difference between $(p_{k+1} - p_k)$ divided by the time video sampling, at the end of the cycle.

When a new frame is acquired, the particles are propagated following state evolution model in correspondence with (Eq. (1)):

$$P_k = AP_{k-1} + Av_{k-1}, \tag{39}$$

$$A = \begin{bmatrix} I_{4x4} & \Delta t.I_{4x4} \\ 0_{4x4} & I_{4x4} \end{bmatrix}, \tag{40}$$

where I_{4x4} is the 4x4 identity matrix, 0_{4x4} is the 4x4 null matrix and Δt is the frame sample time. After the particle propagation the bounds check is applied to verify that all the particles are within the image.

3.3 Particle probabilities estimation

The determination of the similarity between each particle and the reference depends on the type of image, either color or black and white. The images in this text are in black and white from images acquired from infrared sensors, but we will pause here to consider a color image.

3.3.1 Color images

In the case of the color image to determine the similarity with the reference the distance between histograms is used, in the example of the **Figure 6** the Bhattacharyya distance [21] for histograms (Eq. (41)) was used, instead of Euclidean distance, because a better response was obtained.

$$B_{dst} = \frac{\sum\left(hIr - \overline{hIr}\right).\left(hI - \overline{hI}\right)}{\sqrt{\left(\sum\left(hIr - \overline{hIr}\right)^2\right).\left(\sum\left(hI - \overline{hI}\right)^2\right)}} \tag{41}$$

Where B_{dst} is the Bhattacharyya distance, hIr and hI the histogram to be compared, and $\overline{hIr}$ and $\overline{hI}$ its mean values. The probability of one is obtained when the sum of the three distances between the red, green and blue histograms, is equals to zero.

Figure 7 shows the sequence of images for the tracking of a person, in which the particles can be seen in three colors, green for the best estimation, blue for the most probable particles, and red for the least probable ones. At 3.399 seconds the action of the increase dispersion parameter in the resampling procedure is observed, due a low number of valid particles; this is maintained only in two frames, returned to normal values quickly.

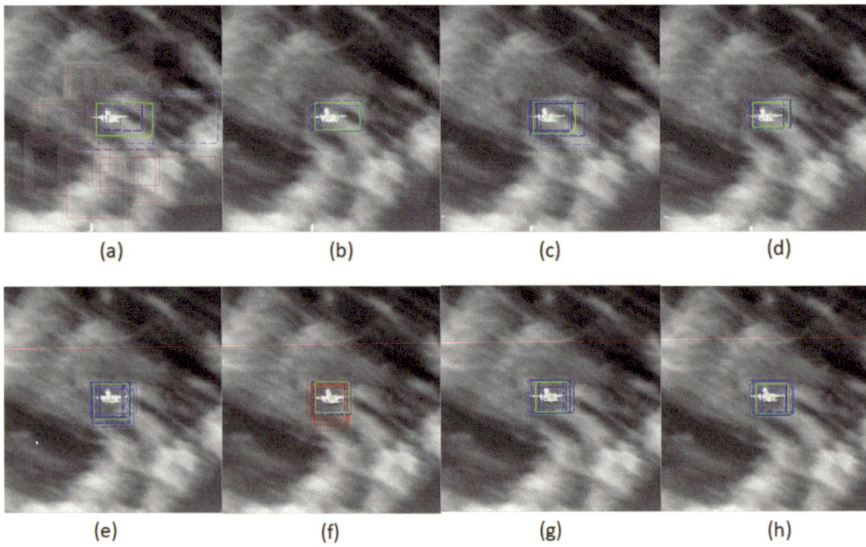

Figure 6.
Airplane sequence of the particle estimator, where [a .. h] correspond to sequences between [4s .. 4.32s].

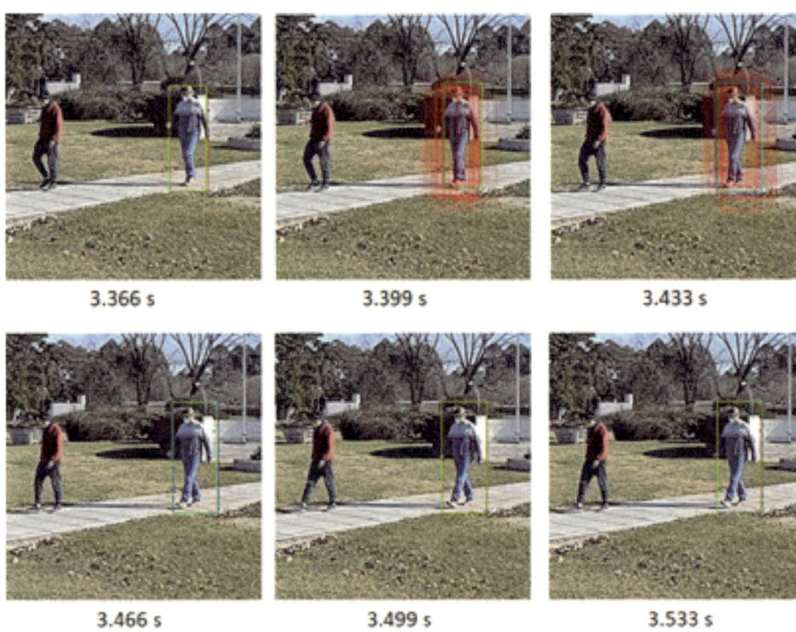

Figure 7.
Person tracking, sequence of the particle estimator.

3.3.2 Black and white images

In the case of the black and white images, for determining the similarity between each particle with the reference, the SURF algorithm was used. Before applying the SURF algorithm, the background effect is reduced, generally this improvement is based on subtracting the value from the mean intensity and modifying its histogram to increase the contrast result a good choice for infrared images. In this case and for this type of image the procedure used to enhance the image of the object was: first subtract the input image I_P by a proportional factor α to its mean value I, second multiply the result by a proportional factor β to the relationship between the standard deviation of the image (as measurement of the contrast) divided by the maximum value of the luminosity (Eq. (42)).

$$I_P = \left[I - \alpha \sum_{i=1,j=1}^{N,M} I_{(i,j)} \right] \beta \frac{\sigma_{(I)}}{\max(I)}, \tag{42}$$

where, N and M are the number of pixels X and Y respectively, $\sigma_{(I)}$ and $\max(I)$ the standard deviation and the maximum value of image respectively. The adaptive factors α and β are obtained experimentally and the best results was obtained with values of $\alpha = 0.84314$ and $\beta = 25$.

For determining the similarity of a particle with the reference particle, a pairing of the characteristic points is performed. After this pairing, the numbers of pairs of points whose metric is less than a threshold metric are counted; and the relationship between the numbers of pairs of points with respect to the total number of characteristic points of the reference particle gives us its similarity probability.

3.4 Position and size of the object to be tracked

The position and size of the object to be tracked is determined by means of the most significant particles, i.e. those particles whose probability exceeds the selected probability threshold.

3.5 Re-sampling

From the most probable particle obtained in the previous step, a new particle set is distributed according to the dispersion of each variable, always limiting them to the size of the screen. But the dispersion of the variables is adapted according to the number of valid particles. This is implemented as a strategy of re-sampling, where the search zone is extended as function of the number of valid particles decreases.

4. Experimental results

Three experimental tests were performed with the previously described algorithm to tracking an object: a) an airplane; b) a six rotors "UAV" and c) a heliport. For the three experiments an infrared camera Tau 640, in the 8 to 14 micron band was used, in a) and b) experiments the camera was mounted on a positioning system, while in c) the camera was mounted on a six-rotor "UAV", taking a zenithal image.

In case b), where the camera was mounted on a positioning system, this had a tracking system attached to it, so the values of the X and Y coordinates in pixels of the target could be obtained. Comparing them with those obtained from the particle estimator the error of the latter was determined.

The images obtained from the video frames were recorded sequentially according to the video acquisition frequency, and before applying the particle estimation algorithm, they were pre-processed by a background suppression and contrast enhancement procedure (Eq. (42)).

In all cases the same observation function, the SURF routine, was used to determine the likelihood of similarity between the video image and the reference image. The dispersion factors applied to the state vector in the resampling function vary inversely proportional to the number of valid particles, so that if the number of valid particles decreases, the search area increases.

4.1 Airplane tracking

The first experiment was the tracking of airplane, the estimator sequence can be observed in **Figure 6**, frame (a) correspond to the first sate of the estimator, distributed the particles over an area of the maximum probability of locate the target.

After the correct detection the particle estimator remains locked throughout the entire flight. As can be observed in frame (f) a lot of particle with probability under the threshold probability appears, but nevertheless remains lock.

4.2 Six rotors tracking

This experiment has the particularity of that the UAV to avoid detection flies hidden behind the trees, after which it starts a free flight. And in both cases the particle estimator is able to detect when only one part of its image visible. From the moment of the first detection the particle estimator remains locked throughout the entire flight. The **Figure 8** shows part of the frames sequence of the flight, from left to right and from top to bottom the "UAV" first flying behind the trees, while the particle estimator begins distributing the particles in the largest possible area of the screen, after the third frame, and with the "UAV" still largely behind the trees, the particle estimator still able to detect it and "hook" it as soon as it partially appears.

From the fourth frame the estimator remains locked during the whole flight, especially when the occlusion free flight is carried out, and the tracking is always right.

4.3 Heliport tracking

This experiment was a flight over a heliport located in a park area of the Institute, and the shots were taken from zenithal videos because an artificial vision navigation system was tested to aid the landing. The characteristics of these images

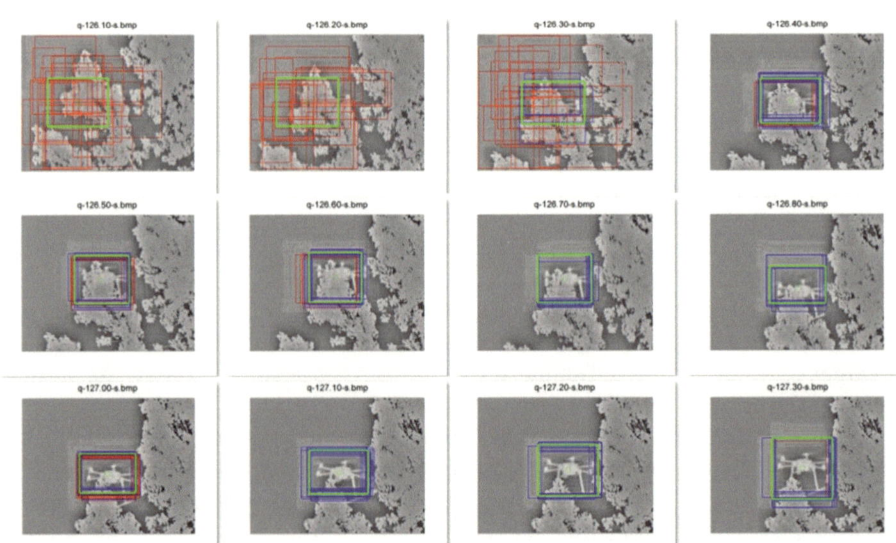

Figure 8.
Six rotors "UAV" sequence of the particle estimator.

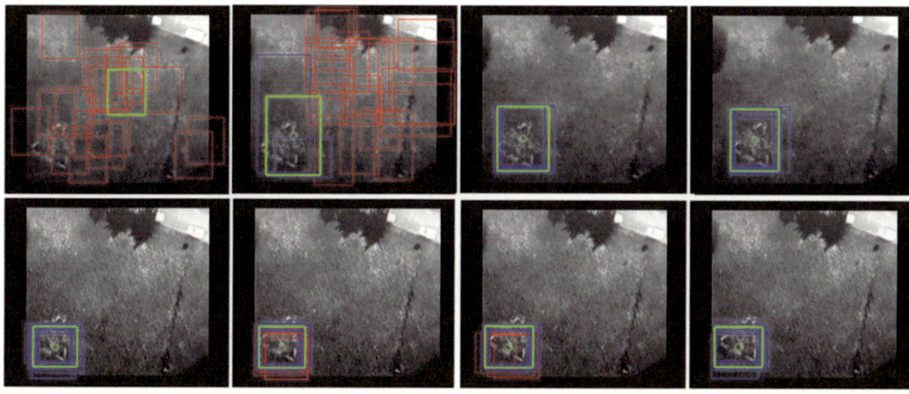

Figure 9.
Heliport tracking sequence of the particle estimator.

are that they are interfered by infrared radiation from the ground, and the heliport is not properly marked.

The **Figure 9** shows two sequences of the particle estimator execution, the upper correspond to the startup, and the lower in the middle of the experiment. From left to right and from top to bottom, the first frame corresponds to the initialization of the estimator, the particles are distributed over the whole image and the most probable particle in the center of the screen. In the second frame after 0.04 seconds (frame rate) only two particles have probability higher than the threshold, and it can be seen how the most probable particle reached the target. After that the estimator is locked, and remains in sequence of tracking.

5. Conclusions

The parameters that define the behavior of the particle estimator were described in paragraph 3. Although an analysis of the estimator's response can be made based on each of these parameters; here we will perform only one, for the number of particles of the estimator.

For this purpose, we rely on the experiment corresponding to the tracking of the six-rotor UAV, because it was simultaneously tracked by a positioning system. Therefore, taking as true the observation obtained from the positioning system, it was possible to determine the relative error corresponding to the particle estimator.

To observe the dynamic response and the internal state of the particle estimator, the relative error (upper graph) and the number of valid particles (lower graph) as a function of time were plotted on **Figure 10**.

This figure show the behavior of the estimator, as a function of the number of particles and in different colors, for values of 30 (red), 50 (magenta), 70 (blue) and 90 (green), the time between marks is the acquisition video time, which is 0.050 seconds.

As can be seen always at least a number of 6 frames are needed to begin reach the lock state, and the number of particles parameter does not affect this number to get this state. But when the number of the particles of the estimator it increase, decreases its relative error, increase the computer time process, and presents greater stability to maintain the lock.

Another parameter that improved the particle estimator response is the dispersion multiplying factor of the state variables. This multiplying factor is increased when the number of valid particles decrease, covering a wider area of search in the

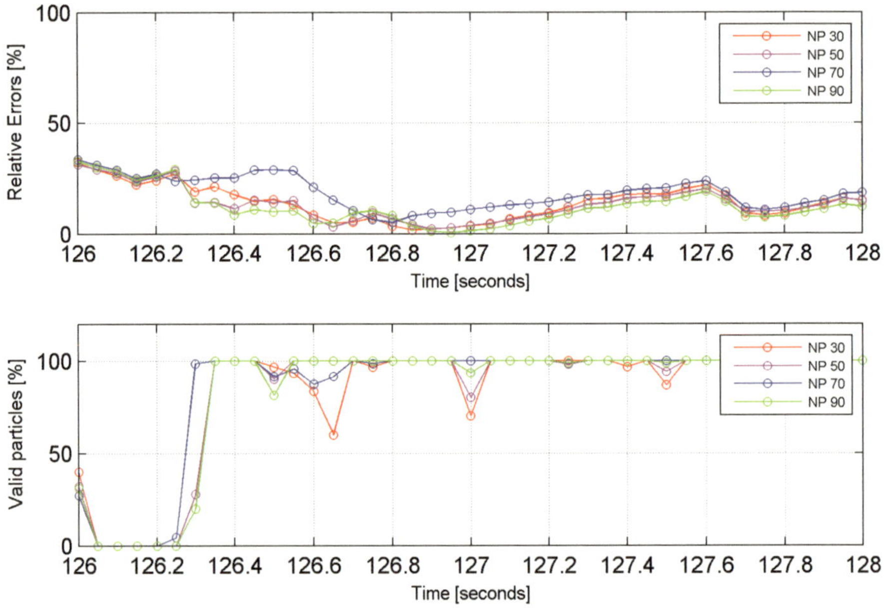

Figure 10.
Dynamic response of the particle estimator.

image. With this search strategy the estimator maintains its stability in the response to the lock with the objective, in a few frames.

After several execution of the algorithm in the experiment b); and varying different initialization parameters of the estimator, the values that produce an acceptable behavior are: number of particles 70 or higher, number of characteristic points of the SURF algorithm 70 or higher, threshold value of probability of similarity 90% or higher.

With the considerations in the initialization parameters of the particle estimator mentioned above, the state lock could be maintained with no more than two frames unlocked. And another observed feature is that the estimator could track the target even when the object is mostly occluded on its surface, for example when the UAV is behind trees (see **Figure 8**).

As a proposed improvement to enhancement to achieve better detection of the target when it is mainly occluded, or when the image is heavily contaminated with noise; it is to reformulate the main strategy. This strategy consists of decomposing the reference image into *NxN* sub-images, in sequence and with their corresponding identification. And for each sub-image a particle estimator is applied, having *NxN* particle estimators, each one looking for a part of the reference image. From there and starting with the first particle, we look for the particles with more probability, and that are located in the correct sequence; the average of these particles will give us the more likely position of the target to be follow. In case that no particles are found in the correct positions we can obtain the most probability position of the object to be followed as the position of the particle with the largest probability, or as the integration of the information provided by the *NxN* estimators.

Acknowledgements

Special thanks to the Post Graduate staff of the National Technological University – Buenos Aires Regional Faculty. And the staff of the Laboratories of the

Institute of Scientific and Technical Research for Defense: Thermal Imaging Laboratory for providing the images of the experience, and to the Digital Techniques Laboratory for carrying out the flight with the unmanned aerial vehicle.

Conflict of interest

The authors declare no conflict of interest.

Author details

Edgardo Comas[1,2]* and Adrián Stácul[1,2]

1 Institute of Scientific and Technical Research for Defense, Buenos Aires, Argentina

2 National Technological University – Buenos Aires Regional Faculty, Buenos Aires, Argentina

*Address all correspondence to: ecomas@frba.utn.edu.ar

References

[1] Maybeck, Peter, Stochastic Models, Estimation and Control, vol. 3. Academic Press, Inc, 1982.

[2] Frank L. Lewis, LIHUA XIE, and Dan Popa, Optimal and Robust Estimation With an Introduction to Stochastic Control Theory, Second. 2008.

[3] David P. Landau, Kurt Binder, A Guide to Monte Carlo Simulations in Statistical Physics, Third Edition. Cambridge University Press, 2009.

[4] Jari Kaipio, Erkki Somersalo, Statistical and Computational Inverse Problems, Vol. 160. Springer Science, 2004.

[5] Arnaud Doucet and Adam M. Johansen, 'A tutorial on particle filtering and smoothing', Handb. Nonlinear Filter., vol. 12, Mar. 2012.

[6] Arnaud Doucet, Simon Godsill and Christophe Andrieu, 'On sequential Monte Carlo sampling methods for Bayesian filtering', Stat. Comput., Jul. 2000, DOI:10.1023/A:1008935410038.

[7] Liu Jun and Chen Rong, 'Sequential Monte Carlo Methods for Dynamic Systems', J. Am. Stat. Assoc., Apr. 1998, DOI:10.1080/01621459.1998.10473765.

[8] Fredrik Gustafsson, 'Particle filter theory and practice with positioning applications', IEEE Aerosp. Electron. Syst. Mag., vol. 25, no. 7, Jul. 2010, DOI: 10.1109/MAES.2010.5546308.

[9] Miroslav Trajkovii, Mark Hedley, 'Fast corner detection', Image Vis. Comput.

[10] Edward Rosten and Tom Drummond, 'Machine Learning for High-Speed Corner Detection'. DOI: 10.1007/11744023_34.

[11] Charles Bibby and Ian Reid, 'Fast Feature Detection with a Graphics Processing Unit Implementation'. University of Oxford, 2006.

[12] Herbert Bay, Tinne Tuytelaars, and Luc Van Gool, 'speeded up robust features', Comput. Vis. Image Underst., vol. 110, no. 3, Jun. 2008, DOI:10.1016/j.cviu.2007.09.014.

[13] H. Kandil and A. Atwan, 'A comparative study between SIFT-particle and SURF-particle', Int. J. Signal Process. Pattern Recognit., Vol. 5, no. No 3, Sep. 2012.

[14] Edward Rosten and Tom Drummond., 'Fusing points and lines for high performance tracking', in IEEE International Conference on Computer Vision, Oct. 2005, vol. Volume 2.

[15] Edward Rosten, Reid Porter, and Tom Drummond, 'A Machine Learning Approach to Corner Detection', IEEE Trans Pattern Anal. Mach. Intell., 2010.

[16] Motilal Agrawal, Kurt Konolige, and Morten Rufus Blas, 'CenSurE: Center Surround Extremas for Realtime Feature Detection and Matching', Oct. 2008. DOI:10.1007/978-3-540-88693-8_8.

[17] Mosalam Ebrahimi and Walterio Mayol-Cuevas, 'Speeded Up Surround Extrema Feature Detector and Descriptor for Realtime Applications', Jun. 2009.

[18] C. Harris and M. Stephens, 'A Combined Corner and Edge Detector', Presented at the Alvey Vision Conference, 1988. DOI:10.5244/C.2.23.

[19] Paul L. Rosin, 'measuring corner properties', Comput. Vis. Image Underst., 1999, DOI:10.1006/cviu.1998.0719.

[20] Vincent Lepetit, Pascal Fua and Christoph Strecha, 'Binary Robust Independent Elementary Features',

CVLab, EPFL, Lausanne, Switzerland, May 2014. DOI:10.1007/978-3-642-15561-1_56.

[21] Briñez de León, Juan CRetrepo Martinez, Alejandro López Giraldo, Francisco E., 'Métricas de Similitud Aplicadas para Análisis de Imágenes de Fotoelasticidad', Dyna, 2013 [Online]. Available: https://www.redalyc.org/articulo.oa?id=49627363006

Chapter 4

Performance Analysis of OpenCL and CUDA Programming Models for the High Efficiency Video Coding

Randa Khemiri, Soulef Bouaafia, Asma Bahba, Maha Nasr and Fatma Ezahra Sayadi

Abstract

In Motion estimation (ME), the block matching algorithms have a great potential of parallelism. This process of the best match is performed by computing the similarity for each block position inside the search area, using a similarity metric, such as Sum of Absolute Differences (SAD). It is used in the various steps of motion estimation algorithms. Moreover, it can be parallelized using Graphics Processing Unit (GPU) since the computation algorithm of each block pixels is similar, thus offering better results. In this work a fixed OpenCL code was performed firstly on several architectures as CPU and GPU, secondly a parallel GPU-implementation was proposed with CUDA and OpenCL for the SAD process using block of sizes from 4x4 to 64x64. A comparative study established between execution time on GPU on the same video sequence. The experimental results indicated that GPU OpenCL execution time was better than that of CUDA times with performance ratio that reached the double.

Keywords: HEVC, ME, SAD, GPU, CUDA, OpenCL

1. Introduction

The Graphics Processing Unit (GPU) [1] is a microprocessor present on graphic cards or game consoles. It has a strong parallel framework initially dedicated to accelerating graphics tasks. Having this innovation and programming language General Purpose computation on GPUs (GPGPU) languages such as Compute Unified Device Architecture (CUDA) [2] and Open Computing Language (OpenCL) [3] enabled applications development in many domains.

CUDA is an NVIDIA Corporation programming model that runs only on NVIDIA GPUs. The OpenCL method, an effort of the Khronos Community, is very close to the CUDA method. However, this is a requirement open for parallel programming on various platforms: CPUs, GPUs, Digital Signal Processors (DSPs) and other types of processors. Taking into account that, OpenCL is able to manage several devices. The concept of context makes it possible to deal with this problem. A context designates a set of devices.

 IntechOpen

However, there are two major differences. The first difference is that OpenCL codes are much larger than CUDA C codes. The multiplatform side of OpenCL explains this. The second difference is that the kernel is built from the host code during runtime using the OpenCL runtime library [4].The OpenCL kernel can be used in two ways, expressly defining the working group's local and global size and the local size or indirectly leaving OpenCL to select its global size of working group. The size of a working group equals a CUDA thread size block, the size of a working group is also known as ND Range configuration, as seen in **Figure 1**.

The two languages provide similar hierarchical decomposition of the computation index space explained on **Table 1**. The synchronization is available on thread block/ work-group level only.

This paper proposed an implementation of the Sum of Absolute Differences (SAD) of the High Efficiency Video Coding (HEVC) Motion Estimation (ME) algorithm on an NVIDIA GPU using CUDA and OpenCL languages to compare their performances.

This manuscript is structured as follows: Section 2 introduces the HEVC SAD algorithm. In Section 3, an overview of ME is given. Section 4 gives and describes the SAD kernel proposed. In Section 4 the experimental results and the discussion are given. Finally, Section 5 concludes this paper.

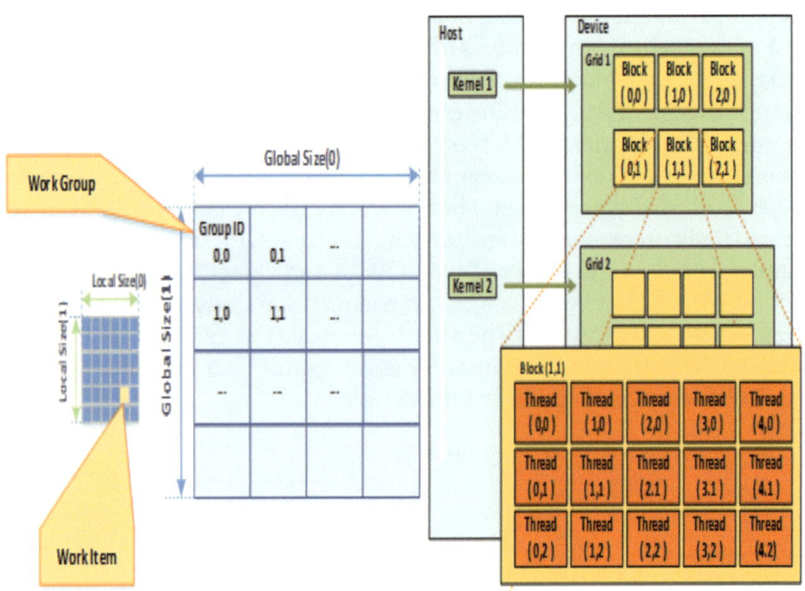

Figure 1.
Model of software programming.

CUDA	OpenCL
Grid	NDRange
Thread Block	Work group
Thread	Work item
Thread ID	Global ID
Block index	Block ID

Table 1.
Execution model terminology mapping.

2. HEVC ME feature

The key element of HEVC is the ME, which represent the most time-consuming task in video coding. Actually, the complexity of ME increases significantly due to the increase in the coding block size [5]. Inter-prediction requires a great complexity burden of up to 80% [6] in the total encoding process, due to the ME, which consumes around 70% of the inter-prediction time, as mentioned **Figure 2** [6].

ME is performed on a block-by-block basis and supports variable block sizes in HEVC. This coding tree unit (CTU) structure, which offers a compromise between a good quality and a less bit-rate, is based on three new concepts: coding unit (CU), prediction unit (PU), and transform unit (TU) [7, 8].

Each picture is divided into CTU of size 64 × 64 pixels, which can be partitioned after that into 4 CUs [9] sized from 8 × 8 to 64 × 64 pixels. These regions of CU contain one or several PUs and TUs.

In the HEVC ME algorithm, SAD and SSD are the most requested functions. These several cost functions are used to decide the best coding mode and its associated parameters. An idea of the SAD is given in the next subsection.

3. HEVC SAD algorithm

The calculation of the Sum of Absolute Difference (SAD) is commonly used for motion estimation in video coding. This is usually the computational intensive part of video processing [10, 11]. It computes the difference between the pixel intensity of the current and reference frame macro block. The motion compensation block size is N × N, where, $Current_{i,j}$, and $Reference_{i,j}$ are current and reference frame block [12].

$$SAD = \sum_{i=0}^{N-1}\sum_{j=0}^{N-1}\left|Current_{i,j} - Reference_{i,j}\right| \tag{1}$$

SAD is also used as an error calculation in order to define the similar block and to evaluate the motion vector in the motion estimation phase [13]. SAD is a simple and fast evaluation metric. This calculation takes every pixel in a block into an account. For many motion estimation algorithms, it is therefore very efficient (**Figure 3**).

4. Proposed SAD kernel

The calculation of the SAD can be parallelized using GUP since it treats each pixel separately, which corresponds to the architecture of the graphics processors

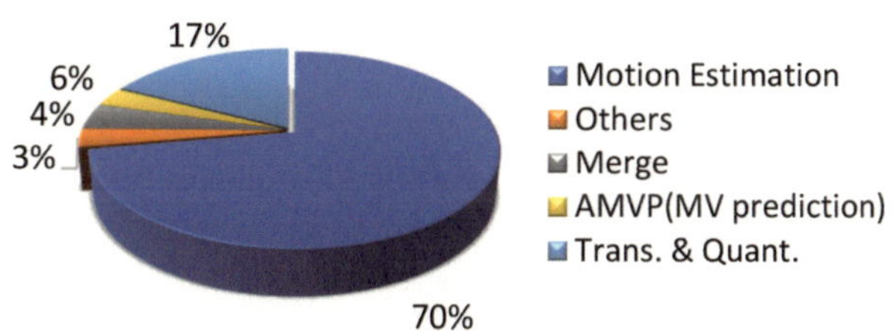

Figure 2.
HEVC inter-prediction time distribution [6].

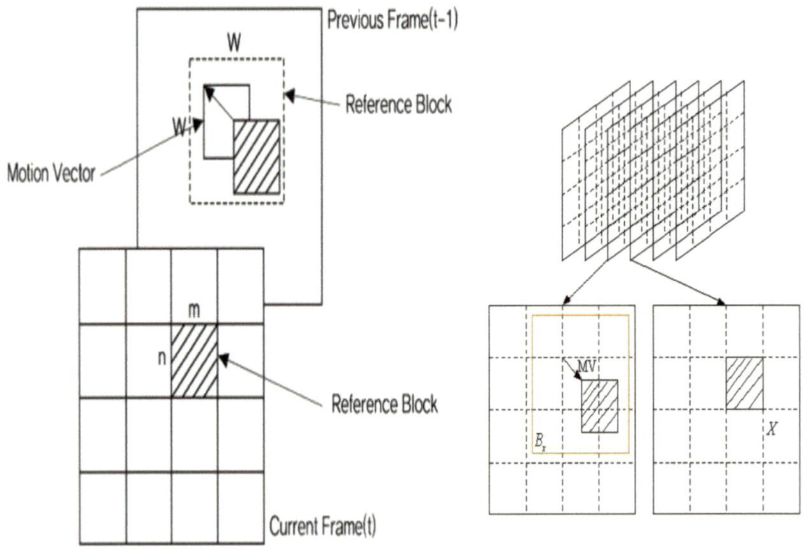

Figure 3.
Block matching algorithm based on SAD.

2D-grid of threads blocks which computes all disparities for 2D blocks of the image. Each thread computes the SAD value for a block in the search range, and a thread block calculates the entire SAD value for an image block. The benefit is that all SADs are calculated in the same thread block for an image block.

In [14] the authors implemented the SAD on the general purpose GPU architecture. A significant acceleration of 204x for an image size of 1024 × 768 was obtained for SAD on the GeeForce GTX 280 compared to the serial implementation as shown in **Figure 4**.

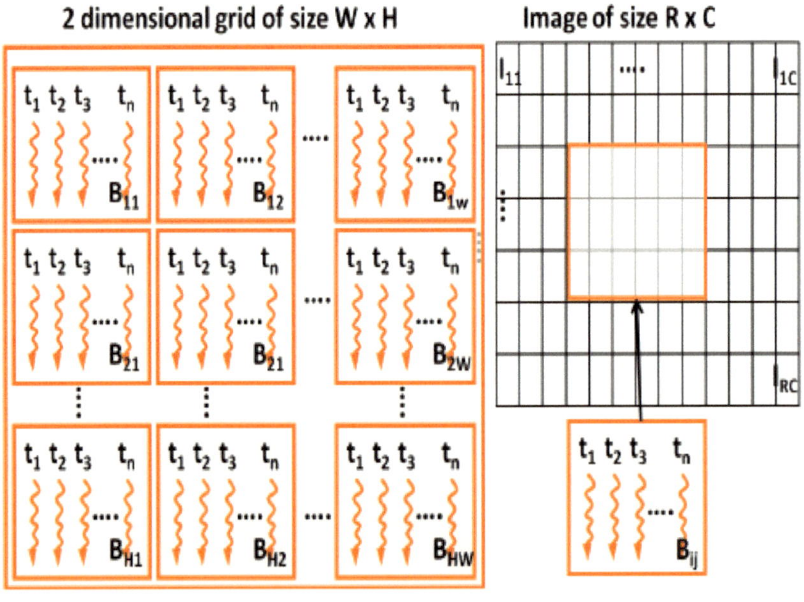

Figure 4.
Typical mapping of a block-matching algorithm to a GPU.

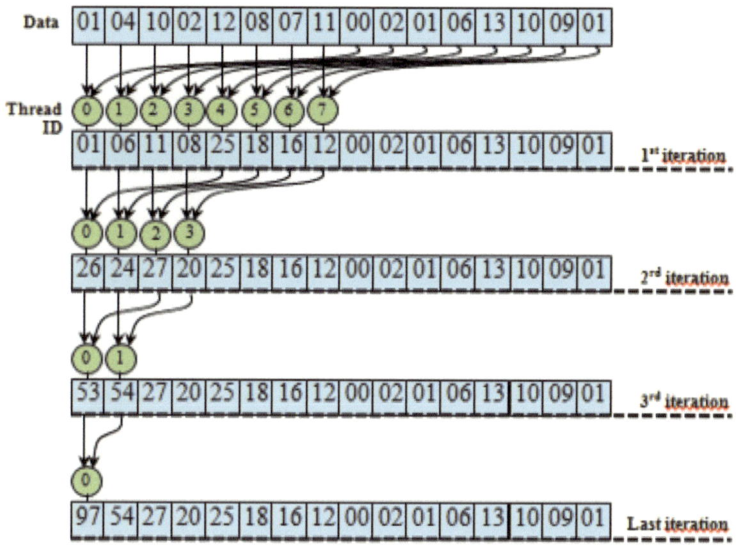

Figure 5.
Reduction technique.

The SAD kernel is composed of two main steps. The subtraction of the PU pixels then the summation. The addition was achieved on the GPU with the parallel reduction. In step1, the first N/2 elements are added to the other N/2. In the result, in the step 2, we have N/2 elements to add up. The first half was added to the next half. The same steps are repeated until there is only one number remaining as shown in **Figure 5** [15].

5. Experimental results

5.1 OpenCL performance on GPU compared the CPU one

OpenCL offers a convenient way to construct heterogeneous computing systems and opportunities to improve parallel application performance. As first step, the OpenCL SAD kernel was implemented in two platforms: CPU with 4 cores at frequency 2.5 GHz and an NVDIA GPU 920 m of 954 MHz as frequency. The SAD block dimensions are from 4×8 to 64×64 pixels. A comparative analysis was made on the same video between the CPU and GPU is seen in **Figure 6**. It is clear from the next figure that the GPU execution time is greater than CPU execution (**Figure** 7) [16].

When using the Eq. (2), **Figure 6** indicates the speed up [17] of the both implementations.

$$Speed - up = CPU\ execution\ time / GPU\ execution\ time \tag{2}$$

The speed up shows that the GPU platform is more efficient than the CPU platform, and this is due to the efficient parallel architecture of GPU compared to CPU. To validate the OpenCL code compared to the CUDA code the next study is proposed.

5.2 Execution performance OpenCL GPU compared to CUDA GPU

Running the application through GPU requires these steps as it is shown in **Figure 8**. For OpenCL, approach contains GPU detection and kernel compilation.

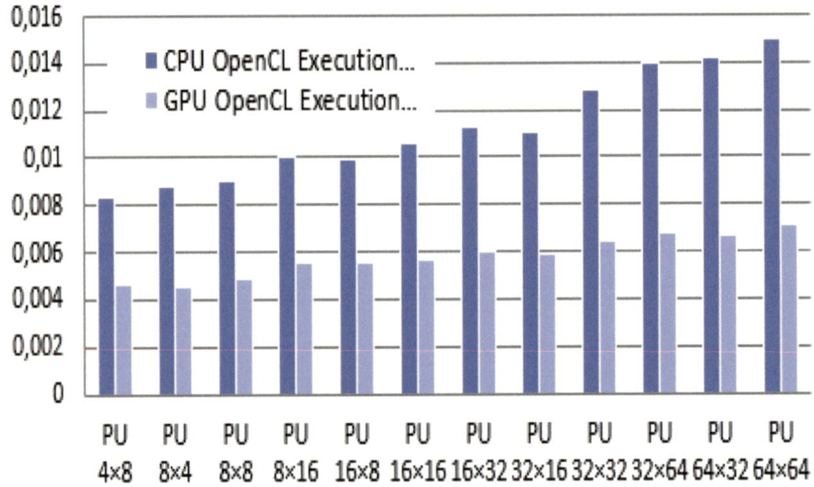

Figure 6.
Performance OpenCL comparison with GPU and CPU platforms.

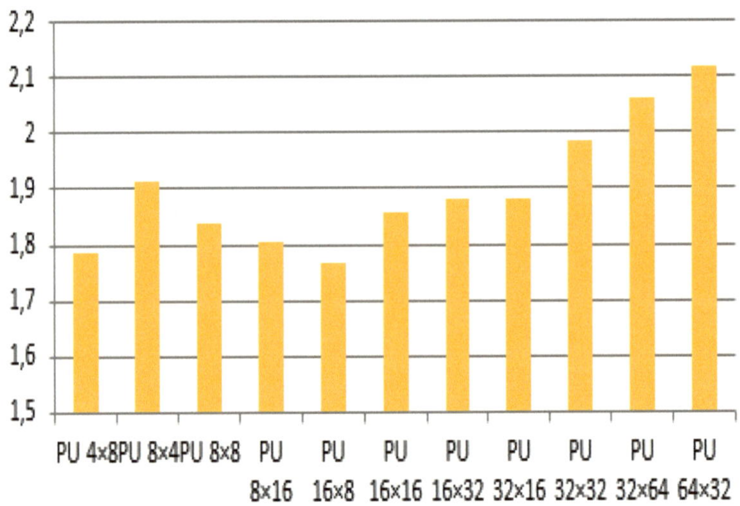

Figure 7.
Speed-up using OpenCL language.

The CPU input is read from the host to the device by all frameworks; the kernel is executed on the GPU; the device is returned to the host by copy data. Finally, the results are displayed on CPU.

Table 2 reports the kernel running time for different size of Prediction Unit (PU) (designed the block size used). In order to get repeated average times, we fixed each problem 10 times for both CUDA and OpenCL.

We use a normalized performance metric, called Performance (PR), to compare the performance of CUDA and OpenCL (**Figure 9**).

$$PR = CUDA \text{ execution time}/OpenCL \text{ execution time} \tag{3}$$

If performance ratio is greater than 1, OpenCL will give a better results compared to CUDA language. As shown in **Figure 8**, the performance ratio indicates that the OpenCL kernel running time is better than CUDA kernel running for each

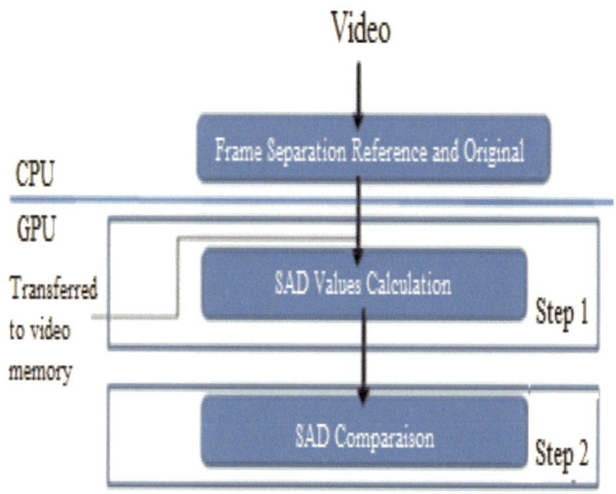

Figure 8.
Algorithm flow.

Block sizes		GPU execution time (μs)	
		CUDA language	OpenCL language
CU 8 × 8	PU 4 × 8	6.63	5.592
	PU 8 × 4	6.885	5.482
	PU 8 × 8	7.573	5.831
CU 16 × 16	PU 8 × 16	8.224	6.013
	PU 16 × 8	8.402	5.909
	PU 16 × 16	8.992	6.356
CU 32 × 32	PU 16 × 32	10.17	6.451
	PU 32 × 16	9.037	6.503
	PU 32 × 32	9.729	6.877
CU 64 × 64	PU 32 × 64	10.265	7.964
	PU 64 × 32	13.1	7.297
	PU 64 × 64	13.687	8.614

Table 2.
GPU and CPU application running times in seconds.

size block. Similar results are obtained by Frang et al. [18] and Exterman [19], respectively.

5.3 Comparative study

In this section, we compared the time performance of our proposed implementation to State-of-the-Art process [20, 21].

In the work presented by Xiao et al. [20], when comparing the result of the proposed with the HEVC reference software, experimental results show that the proposed GPU implementation achieves 34.4% encoding time reduction on average while the BD-rate increase is only about 2% for a typical low delay setting. Another interesting work is proposed by Karimi et al. [21] used a specific real-world application to compare the performance of CUDA with NVIDIA's implementation of

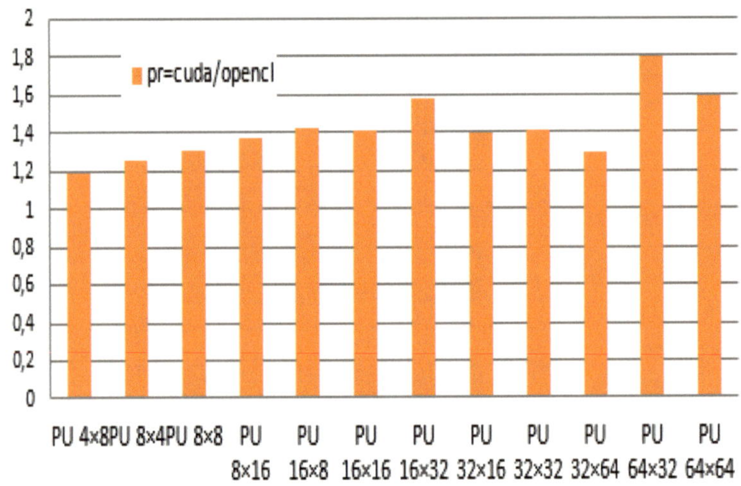

Figure 9.
Performance ratio.

OpenCL. Contrary to our results, CUDA's kernel execution was here consistently faster than OpenCl's, despite the two implementations running nearly identical code. CUDA seems to be a better choice for applications where achieving as high a performance as possible is important. Otherwise the choice between OpenCL and CUDA can be made by considering factors such as prior familiarity with either system, or available development tools for the target GPU hardware. The performance will be dependent on some variables, including code quality, algorithm type and hardware type.

6. Conclusion

OpenCL is quite competitive with CUDA on the NVIDIA graphics processor in terms of performance. In this work, the use of OpenCL as a portable language for the development of GPGPU applications was studied. SAD is the largest part of runtime and calculation in motion estimation the reduction technique was used to implement the SAD, which significantly allows reducing the run time. The performance ratio was equals to 2 when comparing the OpenCL implementation to the CUDA one.

Paralleling multiple GPU algorithms could improve performance. In addition to the ME algorithm of the Joint Collaborative Video Coding Team (JCT-VC) [22], we assume that the suggested concept can also be applied.

Conflict of interest

The authors declare no competing interests.

DOI: http://dx.doi.org/10.5772/intechopen.99823

Author details

Randa Khemiri[1,2]*, Soulef Bouaafia[1], Asma Bahba[3], Maha Nasr[3] and Fatma Ezahra Sayadi[3]

1 Faculty of Sciences, Electronics and Microelectronics Laboratory, University of Monastir, Monastir, Tunisia

2 Higher Institute of Computer Science and Multimedia Gabes, University of Gabes, Tunisia

3 Networked Objects, Control, and Communication Systems Laboratory (NOCCS), National Engineering School of Sousse, University of Sousse, Sousse, Tunisia

*Address all correspondence to: randa.khemiri@gmail.com

References

[1] Osama, M., Wijs, A.: Parallel SAT Simplification on GPU Architectures. In: Vojnar T., Zhang L. (eds) Tools and Algorithms for the Construction and Analysis of Systems. TACAS. Lecture Notes in Computer Science, 114(27) (2019).

[2] Yang, X., Jian, L., Wu, W. et al. J Real-Time Image Proc, https://doi.org/10.1007/s11554-018-0803-y, 2019.

[3] Karimi, K., Dickson, N. G., Hamze, F.: A Performance Comparison of CUDA and OpenCL (2010).

[4] Tsuchiyama, R., Nakamura, T., Iizuka, T., Asahara, A.: The OpenCL Programming Book. Fixstars Corporation (2010).

[5] Richardson, I.: 'HEVC an introduction to high efficiency video coding', VCodexVideo Compression, h ttp://vcodex.com/, accessed 15 January 2016.

[6] Kim, J., Jun, D.S., Jeong, S., et al.: 'An SAD-based selective bi-prediction method for fast motion estimation in high efficiency video coding', ETRI J., 2012, 34, (5), pp. 753–758.

[7] Tai, S., Chang, C., Chen, B., et al.: 'Speeding up the decisions of quad-tree structures and coding modes for HEVC coding units', Adv. Intell. Syst. Appl. (SIST 21), 2013, 2, pp. 393–401.

[8] Hyang-Mi, Y., Jae-Won, S.: 'Fast coding unit decision algorithm based on inter and intra prediction unit termination for HEVC'. IEEE Int. Conf. Consumer Electronics (ICCE), Las Vegas, 2013, pp. 300–301.

[9] Khemiri, R., Bahri, N., Belghith, F., Bouaafia, S., Sayadi, F.E., Atri, M., Masmoudi, N. : 'Fast Motion Estimation's Configuration Using Diamond Pattern and ECU, CFM, and ESD Modes for Reducing HEVC Computational Complexity'. In book: Digital Imaging. Publisher: IntechOpen, pp. 1-18.

[10] Praveen, K., Kannappan, P., Ankush, M., Guna, S.: Parallel Blob Extraction using Multicore Cell Processor. Advanced Concepts for Intelligent Vision Systems (ACIVS), 320–332 (2009).

[11] Vanne, J., Aho, E., Hamalainen, T. D., Kuusilinna, K.: A High-Performance Sum of Absolute Difference Implementation for Motion Estimation," Circuits and Systems for Video Technology, IEEE Transactions on, 16 (7), 876-883 (2006).

[12] The individual procedures of OpenCL: processing program coding, separating individual tasks and transferring them to the respective processors. © Khronos-Group.

[13] Junaid, T., Sam, K., Hui, Y.: HEVC intra mode selection based on Rate Distortion (RD) cost and Sum of Absolute Difference (SAD), Journal of Visual Communication and Image Representation, 35, 112-119 (2016).

[14] Jinglin, Z., Jean François, N., Jean-Gabriel, C.: Implementation of Motion Estimation Based On Heterogeneous Parallel Computing System withOpenc. 14th Ieee International Conference On High Performance Computing and Communications (HPCC), Liverpool, United Kingdom (2012).

[15] Khemiri, R., Kibeya, H., Sayadi, F. E., Bahri, N., Atri, M., Masmoudi, N.: Optimization of HEVC motion estimation exploiting SAD and SSD GPU-based implementation. IET Image Processing, 12(2), 243-253 (2018).

[16] Khemiri, R., Chouchene, M., Barhi, H., et al.: Fast SAD algorithm of HEVC

video encoder on two successive GPU generations', Int. J. Imaging Robot, 17, (2), 1–11 (2017).

[17] Chouchene, M., Sayadi, F., Bahri, H., Dubois, J., Miteran, J., Atri. M.: Optimized Parallel Implementation of Face Detection based on GPU component. Microprocessors and Microsystems, 393–404 (2015).

[18] Jianbin, F., Ana Lucia, V., Henk, S.: A Comprehensive Performance Comparison of CUDA and OpenCL. International Conference on Parallel Processing, ICPP Taipei, Taiwan (2011).

[19] Exterman, D.: CUDA vs OpenCL: Which to Use for GPU Programming, (2021).

[20] Xiao, W., Wu, F., Xu, J., Shi, G.: Fast HEVC Encoding with GPU Assisted Reference Picture Selection, In: Huet B., Ngo CW., Tang J., Zhou ZH., Hauptmann A.G., Yan S. (eds) Advances in Multimedia Information Processing – PCM 2013. PCM 2013. Lecture Notes in Computer Science, Springer, 8294, https://doi.org/10.1007/978-3-319-03731-8_22 (2013).

[21] Karimi, K., Dickson, N. G., Hamze F., A Performance Comparison of CUDA and OpenCL, Cornell University, https://arxiv.org/abs/1005.2581 (2011).

[22] The Joint Collaborative Team on Video Coding (JCT-VC) https://hevc.hhi.fraunhofer.de/.

Chapter 5

Weighted Module Linear Regression Classifications for Partially-Occluded Face Recognition

Wei-Jong Yang, Cheng-Yu Lo, Pau-Choo Chung and Jar Ferr Yang

Abstract

Face images with partially-occluded areas create huge deteriorated problems for face recognition systems. Linear regression classification (LRC) is a simple and powerful approach for face recognition, of course, it cannot perform well under occlusion situations as well. By segmenting the face image into small subfaces, called modules, the LRC system could achieve some improvements by selecting the best non-occluded module for face classification. However, the recognition performance will be deteriorated due to the usage of the module, a small portion of the face image. We could further enhance the performance if we can properly identify the occluded modules and utilize all the non-occluded modules as many as possible. In this chapter, we first analyze the texture histogram (TH) of the module and then use the HT difference to measure its occlusion tendency. Thus, based on TH difference, we suggest a general concept of the weighted module face recognition to solve the occlusion problem. Thus, the weighted module linear regression classification method, called WMLRC-TH, is proposed for partially-occluded fact recognition. To evaluate the performances, the proposed WMLRC-TH method, which is tested on AR and FRGC2.0 face databases with several synthesized occlusions, is compared to the well-known face recognition methods and other robust face recognition methods. Experimental results show that the proposed method achieves the best performance for recognize occluded faces. Due to its simplicity in both training and testing phases, a face recognition system based on the WMLRC-TH method is realized on Android phones for fast recognition of occluded faces.

Keywords: face recognition, linear regression classification, occlusion tendency, weighted module face recognition, texture histogram difference

1. Introduction

As the progress of the computer vision and machine learning, person identification and verification for security considerations become practical and play an important role for modern smart living applications. Face recognition for security control has received lot of attentions recently. Designed with a camera, the face recognition becomes a simple and direct way to achieve reliable identification and verification. There are numerous algorithms [1–4] made important contributions to face recognition. These approaches can be divided into two categories, holistic based and modular based methods [5]. The holistic based approaches include the principle component analysis (PCA) [6] and linear discriminant analysis (LDA) [6]. John *et al.* [7] exploiting sparsity representation to improve the recognition rate. On the other hand, the modular based approaches provide more valuable features for face recognition. Naseem *et al.* [8] proposed linear regression classification (LRC) and its modular design to solve occlusion problems. During training stage, the LRC algorithm is to form the regression surface, which has the most fit of the data distribution, of each identify. In the testing stage, the unlabeled face image vector is used to recognize the person by finding the shortest project distance to the regression surface of the identify.

In practical applications, especially in COVID-19 pandemic period, face recognition might encounter diversified challenges such as low resolution, luminous change, facial expression and partial occlusion affected by facial accessories and covering face masks and scarf. For various challenges, there are several improved LRC algorithms proposed in the literatures, such as PCA-based LRC [9], unitary LRC [10], class-specific kernel LRC [11], and sparse representation classifier [12] methods.

Figure 1 shows some examples of partially-occluded faces, where they are partially covered by facial accessories or covering obstacles. Partially occlusion is one of the practical and difficult problems in face recognition [13, 14]. Thus, some researches have focused on partially-occluded faces [15–19] recently. Most approaches tried to detect the testing images in several modules, avoided occlusion area influence the recognition results. The module LRC (MLRC) proposed in [8] is an effective way to solve occlusion issues in facial recognition. The MLRC treats each module equally important, however the occluded modules should be excluded or reduced their contribution for the final classification. Thus, by using regression parameters (RP), our early-version weighted module linear regression classification (WMLRC-PR) [20] is first proposed to enhance the MLRC method. To secure the access of ATM machines, the occluded face detection methods are proposed [21, 22]. By using support vector machine (SVM) to detect the occlusion modules, the LDA face recognition method is performed in the non-occlusion part [23]. By using structured dictionary learning (SDL) method, the SRC face recognition can separate occluded face images [24]. The robust face recognition algorithms based on various features, such as Huber loss [25], local binary feature [26] and topology preserving structure matching (TPSM) [27] are proposed to solve occlusion problems successfully. It is noted that the state-of-the-art CNN approaches [28–31], which need pre-trained by all face images, will not be applicable for partially-occluded face recognition. Besides, the CNN approaches usually need to pre-train the model, any instance increase of new members becomes impossible.

Situations	Sunglasses	Scarf	Sunglasses & Face mask	Partial face
Occluded Facial Images		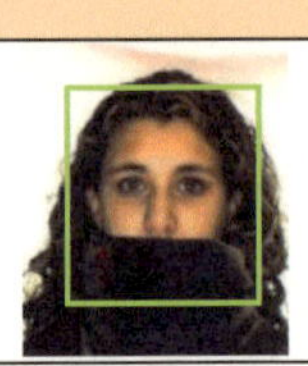		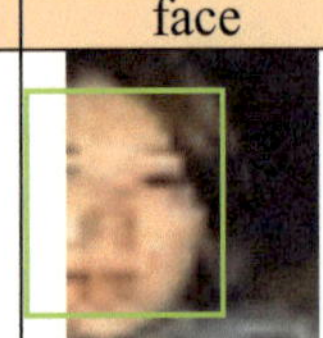

Figure 1.
Examples of partially-occluded situations.

In this chapter, we propose a better occlusion tendency detection by using texture histogram (TH) to distinguish occluded and non-occluded modules. With the TH occlusion tendency, the WMLRC-TH methods are then proposed. The rest of the chapter is organized as follows. In Section 2, we first review the basic LRC concept and introduce the module LRC design for face recognition. Then, Section 3 first analyzes texture histograms and discusses how to use it to determine the occlusion tendency of the module. The proposed WMLRC-TH method in use of texture histogram is the proposed. In Section 4, the proposed WMLRC-TH method, which is tested on AR [32] and FRGC2.0 [33] face databases with synthesized occlusions, is compared to the well-known and robust face recognition methods. The realization of the partially-occluded face recognition system based on the WMLRC-TH method in mobile platforms are also addressed. Finally, conclusions are addressed in Section 6.

2. Module linear regression classification for face recognition

For face recognition, we assume that all training and testing facial images are preprocessed by face detection, face cropping and possible face alignment functions. Assume that we have C subjects, which are characterized by training facial images used for identity recognition. For C identities, the ith identity is with N training facial images all with the size of $p \times q$ pixels. Each pixel could be further represented with K color channels. Thus, the kth channel data of the ith identity is represented by $\boldsymbol{v}_{i,j,k} \in R^{p \times q}$, $i = 1, 2, \dots, C$, $j = 1, 2, \dots, N$ and $k = 1, 2, \dots, K$, where $K = 3$ for most RGB face images.

For the kth channel, we can cascade its q column vectors into a larger column vector, $\boldsymbol{x}_{i,j,k} \in R^{pq \times 1}$. For the ith class identify, its N training vectors, $\boldsymbol{x}_{i,j,k}$, $j = 1, 2, \dots, N$ are grouped into the ith class vector space as

$$\mathbf{X}_{i,k} = [\mathbf{x}_{i,1,k}, \mathbf{x}_{i,2,k}, \dots, \mathbf{x}_{i,N,k}] \in R^{pq \times N}, \quad i = 1, 2, \dots, C. \tag{1}$$

If $\boldsymbol{\nu}_{i,j,k}$ is reformed by linearly combining channels to one grayscale channel, we set $K = 1$ or just remove the subscript k as $\boldsymbol{x}_{i,j} \in R^{d \times 1}$ and $\mathbf{X}_i \in R^{pq \times N}$ for simplicity. For face recognition, the linear regression classification (LRC) and module LRC are briefly reviewed as follows.

2.1 Linear regression classification

Let $\boldsymbol{u}_k \in R^{p \times q}$ be the kth channel of an unlabeled query image, which is formed as a column vector $\boldsymbol{y}_k \in R^{pq \times 1}$. If the query data vector $\boldsymbol{y}_k$ belongs to the ith class, the prediction with the linear combination of the ith class vector space can be rewritten as

$$\mathbf{y}_k = \mathbf{X}_{i,k} \boldsymbol{\beta}_{i,k}, \quad i = 1, 2, \dots, C, \tag{2}$$

where $\boldsymbol{\beta}_{i,k} \in R^{N \times 1}$ is the regression parameter vector of the ith class. The optimal regression parameter vector can be solved by the least square optimization and expressed in matrix operations as

$$\boldsymbol{\beta}_{i,k} = \left(\mathbf{X}_{i,k}^T \mathbf{X}_{i,k}\right)^{-1} \mathbf{X}_{i,k}^T \mathbf{y}_k, \quad i = 1, 2, \dots, C. \tag{3}$$

With optimized regression parameter vector, $\boldsymbol{\beta}_{i,k}$, the predicted response vector $\tilde{\mathbf{y}}_{i,k}$ of the kth channel for the ith class can be formed as

$$\tilde{\mathbf{y}}_{i,k} = \mathbf{X}_{i,k}\boldsymbol{\beta}_{i,k}, \quad i = 1, 2, \dots, C. \tag{4}$$

For all C classes, we first compute the kth-channel predicted response vectors. To construct the recognition system, by combining Eq. (3) and Eq. (4) together, we can store the $pq \times pq$ projection matrix of the ith identity as:

$$\mathbf{H}_{i,k} = \mathbf{X}_{i,k}\left(\mathbf{X}_{i,k}^T\mathbf{X}_{i,k}\right)^{-1}\mathbf{X}_{i,k}^T, \quad k = 1, 2, \dots, K. \tag{5}$$

The construction of the ith projection matrix can be treated as the training process of the ith identity. For the trained parameters of all C identities, we need to store Cp^2q^2 coefficients for recognition. The computation of predicted response vector becomes the projection process as

$$\tilde{\mathbf{y}}_{i,k} = \mathbf{H}_{i,k}\mathbf{y}_k, \quad k = 1, 2, \dots, K, \tag{6}$$

which takes about Kp^2q^2 multiplications. For testing all C identities, one identity recognition process, it needs CKp^2q^2 multiplications. To determine the best class, the LRC method chooses the identity, which is with the minimum prediction error of all channels. Thus, the classified identity i^* is determined by minimizing the L2-norm distance between the predicted response vector and the query data vector as

$$i^*{}_{\text{LRC}} = \arg\min_i (d_i), \quad i = 1, 2, \dots, C. \tag{7}$$

where

$$d_i = \sum_{k=1}^{K} \left\|\tilde{\mathbf{y}}_{i,k} - \mathbf{y}_k\right\|_2, \quad i = 1, 2, \dots, C, \tag{8}$$

for K-channel classifications.

2.2 Module linear regression classification (MLRC)

For real applications, if a query sample is partially corrupted or occluded, the LRC algorithm cannot handle these special situations well since the discernible messages are getting less. The module, which is in a small and clean subface, approach can efficiently overcome this problem.

For the module LRC (MLRC), each training image $\nu_{i,j,k} \in R^{p\,\times\,qxK}$ is segmented into M non-overlapped partitions. **Figure 2** shows an example of segmentation of facial images with M = 16. The mth module, as the LRC approach, is formed as a column vector $\mathbf{x}_{i,j,k}^m$, i = 1, 2, …,C, j = 1, 2, …, N, m = 1, 2, …, M. As Subsection 2.1,

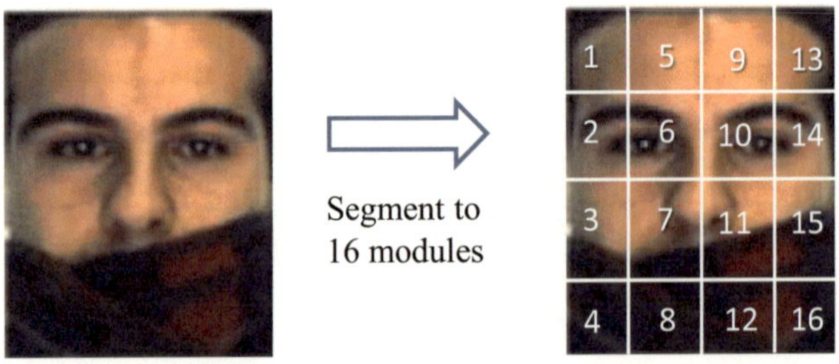

Figure 2.
Segmentation of face images with M = *16 modules.*

in the training phase, the column vectors of all training image related to each class are grouped accordingly. Hence, for the ith class, we could obtain M groups of the kth channel data spaces as

$$\mathbf{X}_{i,k}^{m} = \left[\mathbf{x}_{i,1,k}^{m}, \mathbf{x}_{i,2,k}^{m}, \dots, \mathbf{x}_{i,N,k}^{m}\right] \in R^{\frac{pq}{M}\times N} \tag{9}$$

for $i = 1, 2, \dots, C, j = 1, 2, \dots, N$.

For the kth channel of the query image $\boldsymbol{u}_k$, as the training images, we first segment it to M modules and form them as column vectors $\boldsymbol{y}_k{}^m$ for $m = 1, 2, \dots, M$. If the mth module of the query image, $\boldsymbol{y}_k{}^m$ is assumed to lie on the mth module of the ith class, the least square prediction can be expressed in the training images of the mth module in the ith class as

$$\mathbf{y}_k^m = \mathbf{X}_{i,k}^m \boldsymbol{\beta}_{i,k}^m, \quad i = 1, 2, \dots, C, m = 1, 2, \dots, M, \tag{10}$$

where the optimal regression parameter vector is given as

$$\boldsymbol{\beta}_{i,k}^m = \left(\left(\mathbf{X}_{i,k}^m\right)^{\mathrm{T}} \mathbf{X}_{i,k}^m\right)^{-1} \left(\mathbf{X}_{i,k}^m\right)^{\mathrm{T}} \mathbf{y}_k^m = \mathbf{R}_{i,k}^m \mathbf{y}_k^m. \tag{11}$$

and the regression matrix is defined as

$$\mathbf{R}_{i,k}^m = \left(\left(\mathbf{X}_{i,k}^m\right)^{\mathrm{T}} \mathbf{X}_{i,k}^m\right)^{-1} \left(\mathbf{X}_{i,k}^m\right)^{\mathrm{T}}. \tag{12}$$

Similar to Eq. (5), the corresponding module response vectors $\tilde{\mathbf{y}}_{i,k}^m$ can be predicted as

$$\tilde{\mathbf{y}}_{i,k}^m = \mathbf{X}_{i,k}^m \boldsymbol{\beta}_{i,k}^m = \mathbf{H}_{i,k}^m \mathbf{y}_k^m, \tag{13}$$

where $\mathbf{H}_{i,k}^m$ is the $(pq/M) \times (pq/M)$ projection matrix of the mth module of the ith identity as

$$\mathbf{H}_{i,k}^m = \mathbf{X}_{i,k}^m \left(\left(\mathbf{X}_{i,k}^m\right)^{\mathrm{T}} \mathbf{X}_{i,k}^m\right)^{-1} \left(\mathbf{X}_{i,k}^m\right)^{\mathrm{T}}, \quad k = 1, 2, \dots, K. \tag{14}$$

The project matrix, $\mathbf{H}_{i,k}^m$, for $m = 1, 2, .., M$, $k = 1, 2, \dots, K$ can be treated as the training parameters for the ith identity. For the trained parameters of M modules of all C identities, we need to store CKp^2q^2/M coefficients for recognition process. For testing all C identities, we can directly use (13) to compute the project result. Thus, the MLRC recognition process, which needs to compute all $\tilde{\mathbf{y}}_{i,k}^m$ for M-module and K-channel $p \times q$ facial images by using (13), will need CKp^2q^2/M multiplications. The computation of the MLRC is less than the LRC method, which needs CKp^2q^2 multiplications.

With the above module optimization, each module is processed by the LRC computation individually. Without the knowledge of occluded modules, the minimum distance could be used as the distance metric which implicates that the occluded modules will be automatically removed. The MLRC in min-min distance measure is expressed as.

$$i^*{}_{\text{MLRC}} = \arg\min_i \left(\min_m d_i^m\right), \tag{15}$$

where

$$d_i^m = \sum_{k=1}^{K} \left\| \tilde{\mathbf{y}}_{i,k}^m - \mathbf{y}_k^m \right\|_2, \quad i = 1, 2, \ldots, C; \quad m = 1, 2, \ldots, M. \tag{16}$$

for K-channel classifications.

3. Weighted MLRC by detection of occluded modules

The module linear regression classification (MLRC) shows better recognition performance under occlusion situations. However, the MLRC with min-min distance measure only uses the best module for classification essentially. Thus, we can further improve its classification performance if we can properly gather more reliable non-occluded modules. As shown in **Figure 2**, we should fully utilize all top 8 clear modules (#1, #5, #9, #13, #2, #6, #10, #14) modules and moderately adopt 4 partially-occluded modules (#3, #7, #11, #15) for face recognition.

Thus, in the early age, we suggested an occlusion detection measure, which can be used to infer the occlusion tendency of the module. For linear regression classification method, the occlusion detection could be obtained by regression parameters [15] by the assumption that the regression parameters of the clean modules will have large variations for in-class and out-class faces. The module with small variations of regression parameters will have high probabilities to be detected as the occluded modules. The regression parameter (RP) concept is only good for dark and less texture occlusion objects. If the face recognition algorithm is not a linear regression approach, it will need extra computation to compute the regression parameters. In this chapter, we suggest a simple detection method to find the occlusion tendency of the module. Generally, the module has its particular location, the texture distribution of the module could easily be identified by its texture histogram.

3.1 Occlusion detection by texture histogram

To detect the occluded modules, instead of regression parameters, we can also perform the occlusion detection in the texture domain. First, the D-bin texture histogram of a grayscale image $I(x, y) \in R^{p \times q}$ is expressed by

$$\mathbf{h}_{I(x,y)} = [t_1, \cdots, t_i, \cdots, t_D]^T \tag{17}$$

where the count of gray level $I(x, y)$ for every $b = 256/D$ in D bins will be collected as.

$$t_i = \sum_{y=1}^{p} \sum_{x=1}^{q} q_i(I(x,y)) \tag{18}$$

and $q_i(p)$ is to quantize p into the ith bin as

$$q_i(p) = \begin{cases} 1 \ , & \text{if } (i-1) \cdot b \leq p < i \cdot b \ , \\ 0 \ , & \text{else} \end{cases} \tag{19}$$

For finding D-bin texture histogram of modules of the ith class among N training samples, we first obtain the expected $\boldsymbol{v}^m{}_i$ as

$$\overline{\mathbf{v}}_{i,k}^m = \frac{1}{N} \sum_{j=1}^{N} \mathbf{v}_{i,j,k}^m. \tag{20}$$

where $v^m{}_{i,j,k}$ is the kth channel of the mth module, $v_{i,j,k} \in R^{p \times q}$. Let the kth channel of the query image $u \in R^{p \times q}$, u_k be segmented into M partitions as $u_k{}^m$. To evaluate the occlusion tendency of the modules, $\gamma_i{}^m$, which denotes the distance between the D-bin texture histograms of the mth module of query image $u_k{}^m$ and the averaged module $\overline{\mathbf{v}}_{i,k}^m$ after summing all K channels, becomes

$$\overline{\gamma}_i^m = \sum_k \left| \mathbf{h}_{\mathbf{u}_k^m} - \mathbf{h}_{\overline{\mathbf{v}}_{i,k}^m} \right|_2. \tag{21}$$

It is obvious that the modules of the query image, which are with larger $\overline{\gamma}_i^m$, will have more occlusion tendency due to dissimilar intensity distribution. In AR face database, we test 200 scarf images, With respect to 100 identities, **Figure 3** shows 200x100 overlapped curves of $\overline{\gamma}_i^m$ for all 16 modules. The results also show that $\overline{\gamma}_i^m$ in the occluded modules with m = 4, 8, 12, 16 are larger than the reminding ones. Similarly, the texture histogram difference could be also used to determine the occlusion tendency.

Conceptually, the texture histogram difference (HTD) of the module is a meaningful measure to identify the location of the face. For example, the modules #5 and #6 are forehead and left-center-eye modules, respectively. The average of texture histogram for module #5 has flat texture distribution of pure skin color while that for module #6 is unevenly distributed with textures of eyeball and nose regions. These two modules have their distinct and special texture histograms. If the modules are occluded by the mask, their texture histograms become very different from the original ones. For any face recognition algorithm, the classification criterion generally can be expressed by

$$i^*{}_{\text{face}} = \arg\min_i \left(f_i(\mathbf{y}) \right), \quad i = 1, 2, \dots, C, \tag{22}$$

where $f_i(\mathbf{y})$ denotes the ith class score function of the face recognition algorithm. If we divide the face region into M modules, the adaptive weighted module face recognition algorithm generally becomes

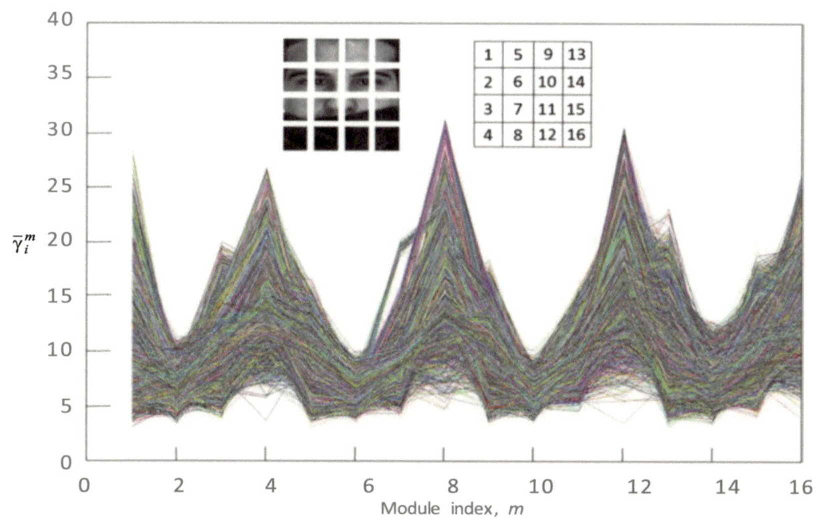

Figure 3.
Plots of $\overline{\gamma}_i^m$ for all 16 modules of 200x100 scarf query images in AR face database.

$$i^*{}_{\text{mface-HT}} = \arg\min_i \left(\sum_{m=1}^{M} g(\bar{\gamma}_i^m) f_i(\mathbf{y}^m) \right), \quad i = 1, 2, \ldots, C, \tag{23}$$

by using the above averaged texture histogram difference stated in (21). In (23), $g(\bar{\gamma}_i^m)$ is a function of HTD parameters should be properly designed to achieve the best face recognition performance. Without loss of generality, we apply the HTD parameters to the adaptive weighted MLRC method in the following subsection.

3.2 Weighted MLRC method by texture histogram

By using texture histogram difference (THD), we suggest a weighted MLRC method, called WMLRC-HT for robust face recognition. For minimization measure errors, it is obvious that occluded modules should give larger weights in the WMLRC such that we can improve the drawback of the MLRC and achieve better recognition performance. Similarly as the observation shown in **Figure 3**, the texture histogram distance, $\bar{\gamma}_i^m$ has highly correlated to the occlusion tendency of the module, In other words, the occluded module has larger $\bar{\gamma}_i^m$ than the normal one. Thus, we define the texture histogram (TH) weight for the mth module to be

$$w_{TH}^m = g(\bar{\gamma}_i^m) = (\bar{\gamma}_i^m)^{-1}. \tag{24}$$

With (24), the TH weight will be bigger for smaller texture histogram difference. Thus, w_{TH}^m for the occluded module is smaller than the normal one.

As the module LRC, the response vector $\tilde{\mathbf{y}}_i^m$ is predicted in terms of $\mathbf{X}_{i,j}^m$ as

$$\tilde{\mathbf{y}}_i^m = \mathbf{X}_i^m \hat{\boldsymbol{\beta}}^m. \tag{25}$$

By using THD weight defined in (24), the WMLRC-TH with the weighted minimum rule can be adjudicated as

$$i^*{}_{TH} = \arg\min_i \left(\sum_m \left(\|\tilde{\mathbf{y}}_i^m - \mathbf{y}^m\| \cdot \frac{w_{TH}^m}{\sum_m w_{TH}^m} \right) \right). \tag{26}$$

4. Experimental results

In our experiments, the recognition performance with different face recognition algorithms will be used to validate the proposed methods. In experiments, AR and FRGC 2.0 face databases are used by synthetically adding osculation. We compare recognition performances of the proposed WMLRC methods to those of PCA, LDA, LRC, MLRC, SRC, locality preserving projection (LPP) [34], neighboring preserving embedding (NPE) [35] methods. All the experiments are carried out on a personal computer, which is equipped with Intel Core2 Q9400 CPU associated a 4-GB RAM. The testing environment is on Microsoft Visual Studio 2013 with OpenCV.

4.1 Experiments on AR database

The famous face recognition algorithms and recent robust face recognition methods [23, 24, 27] all show the recognition performances on AR database, which contains more than 100 people's color face images. For experiments, the cropped facial images are normalized to 40 × 40 pixels. The first experiment is to test all the algorithms on AR database [32] under sunglasses, scarf, colored blocks, black, white, and texture occlusions, overlapped onto normal faces. The AR database consists of more than 100 people's color face images. The images also include several facial variations, such as illumination change, expression and facial disguises. We choose a subset of 100 subjects with 50 men and 50 women. In each subject, 3 normal images are used as the training set as shown in **Figure 4** while 2 images with sunglasses and 2 images with scarf are used for the testing set as shown in **Figure 5**.

Before the experiments, we should first decide suitable settings for the proposed WMLRC-TH method. For module designs, the images are divided into 16 modules, i.e., $M = 16$. For the WMLRC-RP, we choose α, ε, and γ to be fixed to 2, 0.3, 0.7, respectively. The number of bins in texture histogram is $D = 64$ for WMLRC-TH. For the MLRC, we further modify the min-min criterion stated in Eq. (12) to become min-min 4 criterion, the MLRC-4, which is the sum of distances of the best 4 modules as

$$i^*{}_{\text{MLRC-4}} = \arg\min_i \left(\sum_{m*=1}^{4} \min_m d_i^m \right), \tag{27}$$

By using original AR database, **Table 1** shows the comparison results with those normal face algorithms while **Table 2** exhibits the reported results from the recent robust face recognition methods. From **Table 1**, the results show that the proposed WMLRC-TH methods achieved with over 95% accuracy outperforms the other methods. The LDA with SVM method [23] achieves 91.5% recognition rate, the SRC with SDL method [24], the recognition rate for sunglasses plus scarf face images, the recognition rate achieves up to 92%. The topology preserving structure matching (TPSM) [27] achieve 91.7%. recognition accuracy. From **Table 2**, the proposed WMLRC-TH outperforms the WMLRC-RP [20], the LDA-SVM [23], SRC-SDL [24] and TPSM [27] methods for recognizing occlusion face images on AR database.

To further analyze the detailed performances of the algorithms with different conditions of occlusions. The synthesized occlusions with various occlusion levels overlapped to the normal faces are shown in **Figures 6–9**. We still keep all the face

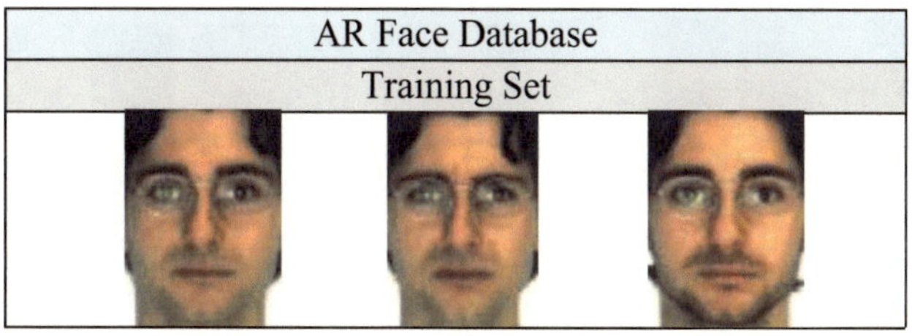

Figure 4.
Normal faces as the training set on AR database.

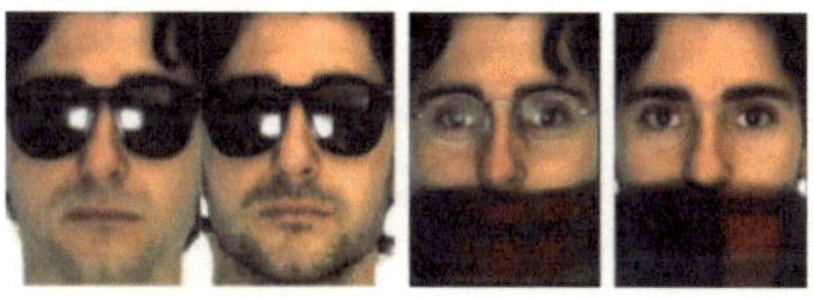

Figure 5.
Sunglasses and scarf occluded faces on AR database.

Situations	Methods					
	PCA	LDA	LPP	NPE	LRC	MLRC
Sunglasses	34.5	28.0	16.5	49.0	64.0	88.0
Scarf	5.0	18.0	12.5	9.0	23.0	45.0
Average	19.75	23.0	14.5	29.0	43.5	65.0
Situations	**Methods**					
	MLRC- 4	**SRC [12]**	**WMLRC-RP [20]**	**WMLRC-TH (K = 1)**	**WMLRC-TH (K = 3)**	
Sunglasses	72.0	93.0	89.0	95.0	97.5	
Scarf	92.0	52.0	87.5	96.0	97.0	
Average	82.0	72.5	88.25	95.5	97.25	

Table 1.
Recognition performances (%) achieved by different methods for sunglasses and scarf images on AR database.

Robust Recognition Methods	WMLRC-RP [20]	LDA-SVM [23]	SRC-SDL [24]	TSPM [27]	WMLRC-TH (K = 3)
Average Recognition Rates	86.0	91.5	92.0	91.7	97.25

Table 2.
Recognition performances (%) achieved by the recently-proposed robust face recognition algorithms on AR database.

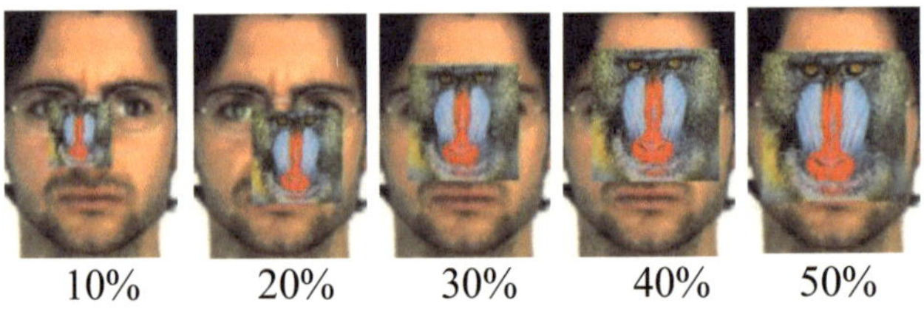

Figure 6.
Added colored occlusion with occlusion ratios on AR database.

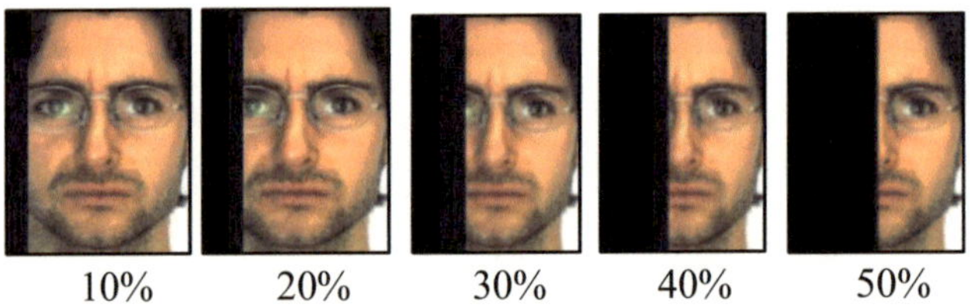

Figure 7.
Black partial occlusion with various occlusion ratios on AR database.

recognition algorithms with same settings, it is noted the synthesized occlusion images are used for the testing results.

Tables 3–6 show the recognition performances of all the face recognition methods for all synthesized occlusion cases, where WMLRC-TH1 and WMLPRC-TH3 denote the WMLRC-TH preformed with gray (K = 1) and RGB color (K = 3) images, respectively. The experimental results show that the proposed WMLRC-TH with gray and color images outperform the other methods, which can achieve over

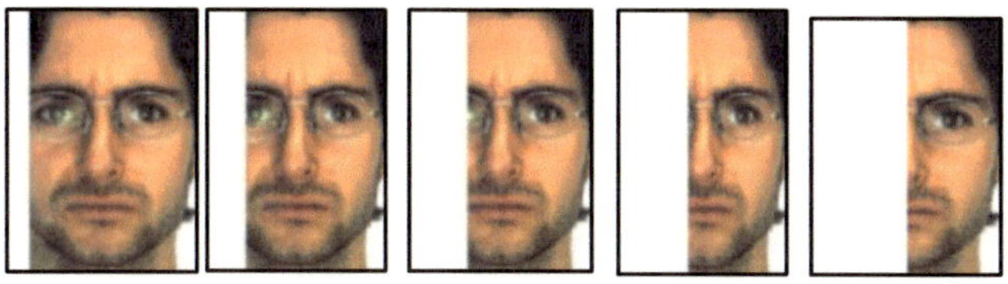

Figure 8.
White partial occlusion with various occlusion ratios on AR database.

Figure 9.
Different occlusion (a) - (e) color wall patterns with 50% occlusion ratio on AR database.

Methods	Occlusion ratio					
	10%	20%	30%	40%	50%	Average
PCA [6]	31.0	16.0	7.0	5.0	3.0	12.4
LDA [7]	40.0	27.0	12.0	11.0	6.0	19.2
LPP	14.0	9.0	5.0	3.0	3.0	6.8
NPE	30.0	20.0	12.0	9.0	7.0	15.6
LRC [8]	50.0	33.0	23.0	11.0	6.0	24.6
SRC [12]	84.0	70.0	70.0	68.0	40.0	66.4
MLRC [8]	87.0	87.0	1.0	1.0	1.0	35.4
MLRC-4	98.0	98.0	1.0	1.0	1.0	39.8
WMLRC-RP [20]	88.0	88.0	88.0	81.0	81.0	85.2
WMLRC-TH (k = 1)	98.0	98.0	98.0	98.0	96.0	97.6
WMLRC-TH (k = 3)	98.0	98.0	98.0	98.0	98.0	98.0

Table 3.
Recognition performances (%) of different methods with varying occlusion ratios of dark partial occlusion on AR database.

95% of accuracy. The MLRC and MLRC-4 performed badly in dark occlusion because low pixel value produces low prediction error, which leads to error recognition. All results show that the proposed WMLRC-TH methods achieve the best recognition performances. The WMLRC-TH had a few benefit from RGB color information since the WMLRC-TH (K = 3) exhibits better recognition performance than WMLRC-TH (K = 1).

4.2 Experiments on FRGC 2.0 database

The second experiments are to test all the methods on the FRGC2.0 database [33, 36] under gray texture blocks, dark, white, and texture occlusions overlapped

Methods	Occlusion ratio					
	10%	20%	30%	40%	50%	Average
PCA	53.0	63.0	61.0	32.0	52.0	52.2
LDA	42.0	67.0	67.0	17.0	20.0	42.6
LPP	21.0	39.0	31.0	11.0	16.0	23.6
NPE	49.0	68.0	61.0	30.0	43.0	50.2
LRC	86.0	53.0	30.0	12.0	6.0	37.4
SRC	96.0	93.0	76.0	68.0	39.0	74.4
MLRC	97.0	97.0	89.0	79.0	39.0	79.4
MLRC-4	97.0	96.0	94.0	70.0	61.0	83.6
WMLRC-RP	91.0	88.0	84.0	81.0	43.0	77.4
WMLRC-TH (k = 1)	98.0	98.0	93.0	85.0	61.0	87.0
WMLRC-TH (k = 3)	98.0	98.0	95.0	86.0	70.0	89.4

Table 4.
Recognition performances (%) of different methods with varying occlusion ratios of colored block occlusion on AR database.

Methods	Occlusion ratio					
	10%	20%	30%	40%	50%	Average
PCA	13.0	9.0	8.0	7.0	2.0	7.2
LDA	23.0	6.0	4.0	8.0	6.0	9.4
LPP	10.0	10.0	5.0	4.0	4.0	6.6
NPE	13.0	6.0	7.0	5.0	5.0	7.2
LRC	28.0	15.0	12.0	12.0	9.0	15.2
SRC	86.0	86.0	70.0	68.0	39.0	83.6
MLRC	87.0	87.0	82.0	82.0	81.0	83.8
MLRC-4	95.0	95.0	95.0	95.0	95.0	95.0
WMLRC-RP	89.0	89.0	84.0	84.0	78.0	84.8
WMLRC-TH (k = 1)	98.0	98.0	95.0	95.0	95.0	96.2
WMLRC-TH (k = 3)	98.0	98.0	95.0	96.0	96.0	97.2

Table 5.
Recognition performances (%) of different methods with varying levels of white partial occlusion on AR database.

onto normal faces. The FRGC2.0 database consists of more than 4000 people's front-view grayscale images including non-facial expressions and slightly facial variations. We choose a subset of 100 subjects with 50 men and 50 women. In each subject, two non-facial expression images are used for the training set as shown in **Figure 10**. In additions, the synthesized occlusions with various occlusion levels overlapped to normal faces as shown in **Figures 11–14** are also used for the testing. As to the experiment settings, the facial images are also normalized to 40×40 pixels and divided into 16 modules.

Tables 7–10 illustrate the recognition performances of all the methods in all test cases. On FRGC 2.0 database, the proposed WMLRC-TH methods also achieve

Methods	Occlusion texture					
	A	B	C	D	E	Average
PCA	20.0	10.0	22.0	12.0	16.0	16.0
LDA	18.0	15.0	19.0	11.0	16.0	15.8
LPP	3.0	4.0	7.0	3.0	4.0	4.2
NPE	17.0	11.0	19.0	13.0	16.0	15.2
LRC	33.0	19.0	34.0	25.0	22.0	26.6
SRC	45.0	40.0	39.0	55.0	39.0	43.6
MLRC	82.0	82.0	82.0	82.0	82.0	82.0
MLRC-4	95.0	95.0	95.0	95.0	95.0	95.0
WMLRC-RP	86.0	86.0	87.0	84.0	85.0	85.6
WMLRC-TH (k = 1)	96.0	94.0	94.0	95.0	95.0	95.4
WMLRC-TH (k = 3)	96.0	94.0	96.0	97.0	95.0	95.6

Table 6.
Recognition performances (%) of different methods with different occlusion textures of 50% occlusion on AR database.

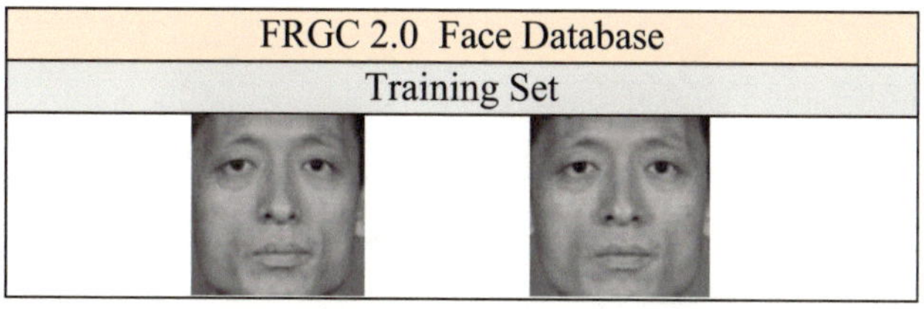

Figure 10.
Normal faces as the raining set on FRGC2.0 database.

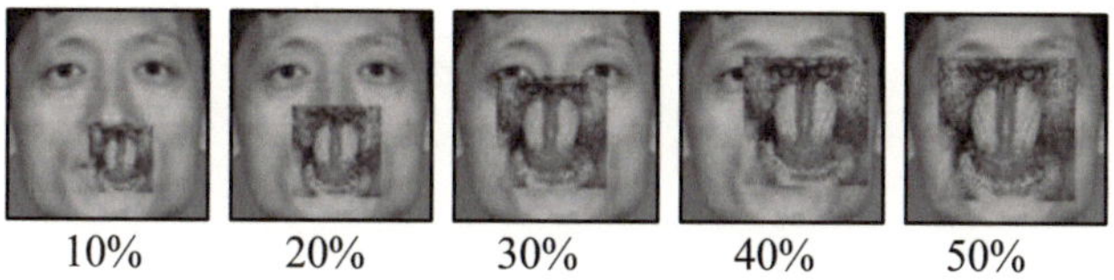

Figure 11.
Added texture block with various occlusion ratios on FRGC 2.0 database.

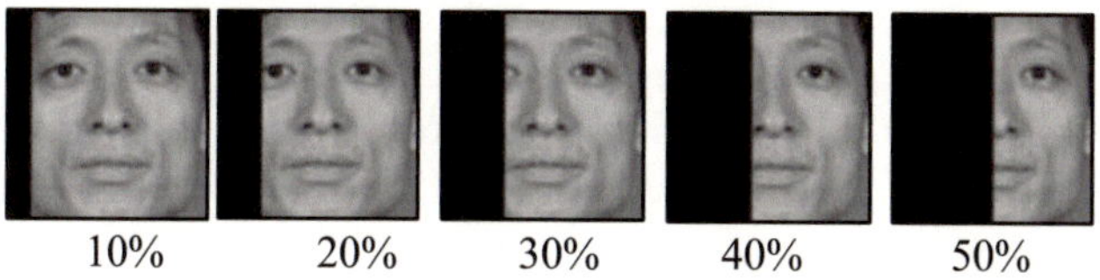

Figure 12.
Dark partial occlusion with various occlusion ratios on FRGC 2.0 database.

better performances than other approaches. From **Table 8**, the MLRC and MLRC-4 performed badly in dark occlusion also. In most cases, the WMLRC-TH performs better than WMLRC-RP. In flat and bright occlusions, as shown in **Table 9**, the WMLRC-RP carries out the better performance than WMLRC-TH. Since the

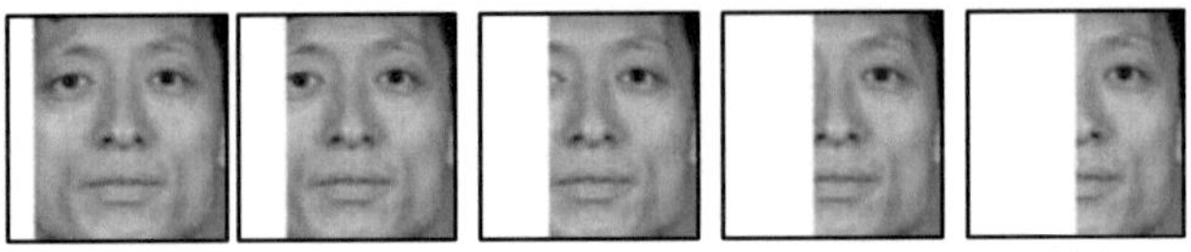

Figure 13.
White partial occlusion with various occlusion ratios on FRGC 2.0 database.

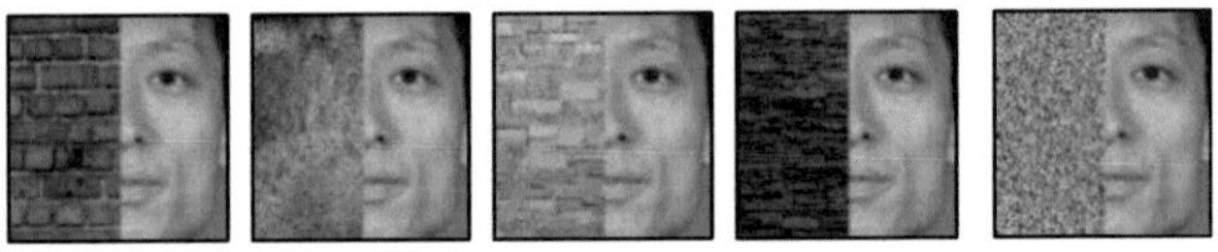

Figure 14.
Different occlusion (a) - (e) gray wall patterns with 50% occlusion on FRGC 2.0 database.

Methods	Occlusion ratio					
	10%	20%	30%	40%	50%	Avg
PCA	99.0	95.0	86.0	61.0	37.0	75.6
LDA	99.0	97.0	81.0	62.0	40.0	75.8
LPP	85.0	64.0	39.0	31.0	14.0	46.6
NPE	98.0	94.0	91.0	76.0	61.0	84.0
LRC	70.0	65.0	52.0	32.0	12.0	46.2
SRC	98.0	92.0	80.0	69.0	42.0	76.2
MLRC	96.0	96.0	97.0	94.0	82.0	93.0
MLRC-4	97.0	96.0	96.0	96.0	89.0	94.8
WMLRC-RP	96.0	90.0	85.0	85.0	82.0	87.6
WMLRC-TH (k = 1)	99.0	98.0	97.0	97.0	92.0	96.6

Table 7.
Recognition performances (%) of different methods with varying occlusion ratios of random block occlusion on FRGC 2.0 database.

sunglasses are the most common situation in daily life, WMLRC-RP is still useful in real applications in the cases of dark occlusions.

From above experiments, the proposed WMLRC-HT method achieves best accurate recognition rate. For the cases of light color occlusions, the WMLRC-RP performs better than the WMLRC-HT. For the other cases, the WMLRC-HT achieves the best recognition performances. The simulations show that the texture histogram feature can be used to detect occluded modules effectively. Besides, we observe that the MLRC-TH in RGB space domain performs better than that in grayscale domain because the grayscale images would waste the useful colored information.

4.3 Android based system implementation

Recently, Android-based operating system successfully supports smartphones and tablets because of its computing ability, storage capacity and its handy

Methods	Occlusion ratio					
	10%	20%	30%	40%	50%	Avg
PCA	63.0	18.0	5.0	4.0	3.0	18.6
LDA	82.0	19.0	22.0	6.0	4.0	26.6
LPP	35.0	32.0	24.0	12.0	6.0	21.8
NPE	40.0	21.0	18.0	9.0	1.0	17.8
LRC	49.0	25.0	14.0	2.0	1.0	18.2
SRC	88.0	86.0	70.0	68.0	41.0	70.6
MLRC	97.0	97.0	1.0	1.0	1.0	39.4
MLRC-4	98.0	98.0	1.0	1.0	1.0	39.8
WMLRC-RP	96.0	96.0	95.0	95.0	95.0	95.4
WMLRC-TH (k = 1)	98.0	98.0	97.0	97.0	97.0	97.4

Table 8.
Recognition performances (%) of different methods with varying occlusion ratios of dark occlusion on FRGC 2.0 database.

Methods	Occlusion ratio					
	10%	20%	30%	40%	50%	Avg
PCA	21.0	7.0	6.0	4.0	2.0	8.0
LDA	36.0	23.0	9.0	8.0	5.0	16.2
LPP	14.0	5.0	2.0	2.0	1.0	4.8
NPE	20.0	15.0	10.0	7.0	4.0	9.8
LRC	25.0	16.0	9.0	4.0	3.0	11.4
SRC	88.0	81.0	46.0	32.0	29.0	55.2
MLRC	97.0	97.0	93.0	93.0	93.0	94.6
MLRC-4	97.0	97.0	97.0	97.0	97.0	97.0
WMLRC-RP	100	100	100	100	100	100.0
WMLRC-TH (k = 1)	98.0	98.0	96.0	97.0	96.0	97.0

Table 9.
Recognition performances (%) of different methods with varying occlusion ratios of white partial occlusion on FRGC 2.0 database.

functions for image capture and image processing. Thus, we realize the proposed WMLRC-TH method on Android system to a robust face recognition system on mobile devices since it has more robust performance in general situations, especially in color image.

In general, the face recognition system can be divided into training phase and the testing phases. As shown in **Figure 15**, the user needs to select the training phase first after capturing face images of a new identity. The user will be asked to enter the name of the identity then the system will store face images with the name in database. In the test phase, the user can capture face image and then identify it. The testing phase basically consists of three steps. **Figure 16** shows the flow chart of testing phase. The first step is the face detection, which rapidly captures human faces when the human is located within a proper distance by the mobile phone camera. The second step is the pre-processing stage that is removing the noisy

Methods	**Occlusion texture**					
	A	**B**	**C**	**D**	**E**	**Avg**
PCA	20.0	36.0	15.0	11.0	26.0	21.6
LDA	14.0	19.0	17.0	14.0	23.0	17.4
LPP	16.0	19.0	6.0	10.0	6.0	11.4
NPE	24.0	33.0	17.0	8.0	20.0	20.4
LRC	34.0	42.0	18.0	7.0	21.0	24.4
SRC	40.0	47.0	45.0	66.0	39.0	47.4
MLRC	93.0	93.0	93.0	93.0	93.0	93.0
MLRC-4	95.0	95.0	95.0	95.0	95.0	95.0
WMLRC-RP	91.0	93.0	92.0	88.0	92.0	91.2
WMLRC-TH (k = 1)	96.0	94.0	95.0	97.0	91.0	94.6

Table 10.
Recognition performances (%) of different methods with different occlusion texture of 50% occlusion on FRGC 2.0 database.

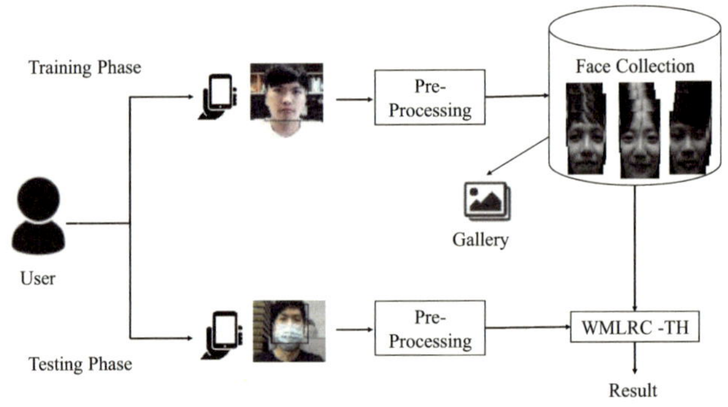

Figure 15.
Proposed android face recognition system.

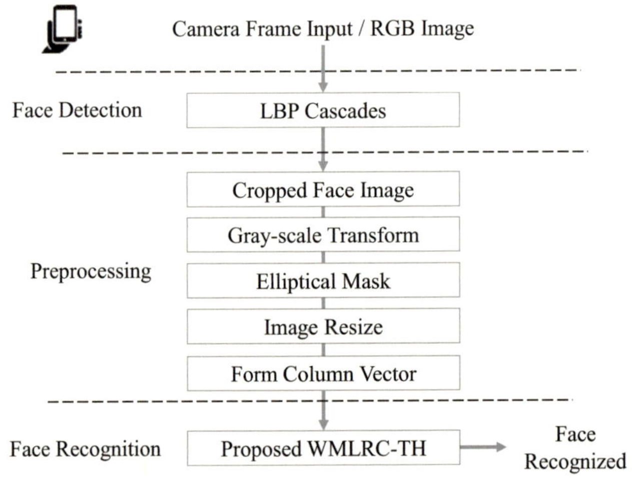

Figure 16.
Flow chart of testing phase in Andorid phones.

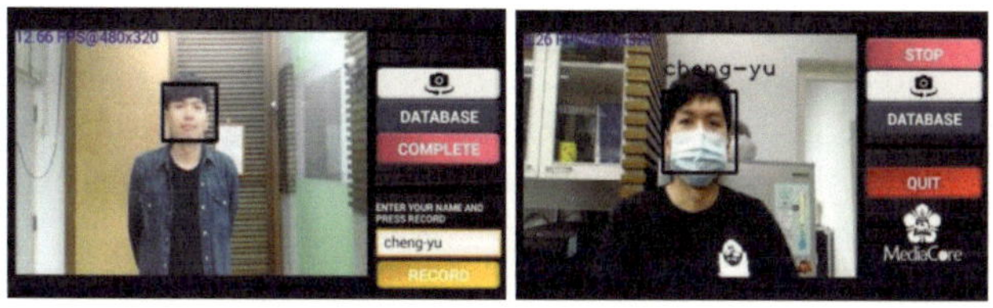

(a) (b)

Figure 17.
User interfaces for registration and face recognition. (a) Registration and setup database (b) recognition and show name.

pixels like background and human hairs of the face images. The third step is face recognition that is recognizing the face according to the face database collected before.

Considering the computation resources of mobile phones, we surveyed several face detection methods [37–41]. By trade-off between accuracy and computation, we finally selected the LBP-feature [37] for face detector, where the LBP operator is given as:

$$LBP(x_c, y_c) = \sum_{p=0}^{P-1} 2^p s(i_p - i_c), s(x) = \begin{cases} 1, x \geq 0 \\ 0, x < 0 \end{cases} \quad (28)$$

where i_c is the intensity of (x_c, y_c), at the central pixel in the local image, i_p is the intensity of neighbor pixel. P is the total number of neighbor pixels. After face detection, the pre-processing stage, including cropping, gray transform, elliptical mask, and resizing. It is noted that the face detection and pre-processing should be identically performed in both training and testing phases. Finally, the face image vector is then classified by the proposed WMLRC-HT algorithm. **Figure 17** shows the user interfaces of face registration and face recognition of the proposed system.

The proposed Android face recognition system is mainly developed on OpenCV SDK and Android NDK (Native Development Kit). Android NDK is used to overcome the limitations of Java, such as memory management and performance, by programming directly into Android native interface to support native development in C/C++.

5. Conclusion

In this chapter, we first review the linear regression classification algorithm as the base of face recognition. If we divide the face region into several subfaces, called modules, any face recognition algorithm will become a new module face recognition algorithm, which can avoid the serious degradation of recognition performance to solve the occlusion problem. We proposed the texture histogram difference of the module to detect the its occlusion tendency of the input face image. The concept of the texture histogram difference can be used for any face recognition algorithms if they adopt the module design. By using texture histogram (HT) concept, the weighted module linear regression classification (WMLRC-HT) method for partially-occluded face recognition is finally proposed. The proposed WMLRC-HT method with adaptive HT weights can effectively improve the shortcoming of the original LRC and MLRC algorithms. The experimental results show that the proposed WMLRC-HT method performs better than the existing linear regression classification methods and the contemporary approaches like SRC with various occluded situations. Since the WMLRC-HT method acquires small computation cost in both training and testing, after the face detector with LBP-features, we implement the proposed method on smart phones. Even the people wear masks, we can easily train and successfully detect the identify only with a smart phone.

Acknowledgements

This work was supported by Ministry of Science and Technology, Taiwan, MOST 110-2221-E-006-119.

Conflict of interest

The authors declare no conflict of interest.

Author details

Wei-Jong Yang, Cheng-Yu Lo, Pau-Choo Chung and Jar Ferr Yang*
Institute of Computer and Communication Engineering, Department of Electrical Engineering, National Cheng Kung University, Tainan, Taiwan

*Address all correspondence to: jefyang@mail.ncku.edu.tw

References

[1] Lu J, Liong VE, Wang G, and P. Moulin. Joint Feature Learning for Face Recognition. IEEE Trans. on Information Forensics and Security. 2015; 10 (7): 1371-1383, July 2015. DOI: 10.1109/TIFS.2015.2408431.

[2] Mery D and Bowyer K. Face Recognition via Adaptive Sparse Representations of Random Patches. In: Proc. of IEEE International Workshop on Information Forensics and Security (WIFS); p. 13-18, 2014. DOI: 10.1109/WIFS.2014.7084296.

[3] Lu J. Liong VE. Zhou X. and Zhou J. Learning Compact Binary Face Descriptor for Face Recognition. IEEE Trans. on Pattern Analysis and Machine Intelligence, 2015 37(10): 2041-2056, 2015. DOI: 10.1109/TPAMI.2015.2408359

[4] Peng X, Zhang L, Yi X and Tan KK. Learning Locality-Constrained Collaborative Representation for Robust Face Recognition. Pattern Recognition, 47(9), pp. 2794-2806, 2014. DOI: 10.1016/j.patcog.2014.03.013

[5] Zou J, Qiang J and Nagy G. A Comparative Study of Local Matching Approach for Face Recognition. IEEE Trans. on Image Processing. 16, (10), pp. 2617–2628, 2007. DOI: 10.1109/TIP.2007.904421.

[6] Martinez AM and Kak AC. PCA versus LDA. IEEE Trans. on Pattern Analysis. and Machine Intelligence. 23 (2), pp. 228-233, 2001. DOI: 10.1109/34.908974.

[7] Wright J, and Yang AY. Robust Face Recognition via Sparse Representation. IEEE Trans. on Pattern Analysis. and Machine Intelligence, 31 (2), pp. 210-227, 2009. DOI: 10.1109/34.908974.

[8] Naseem I, Togneri R and Bennamoun M. Linear Regression for Face Recognition," IEEE Trans. on Pattern Analysis. and Machine Intelligence, 32 (11), pp. 2106-2112, 2010. DOI: 10.1109/TPAMI.2010.128

[9] Huang S and Yang J. Improved Principal Component Regression for Face Recognition under Illumination Variations. IEEE Signal Processing Letters, 19 (4), pp. 179-182, 2012. DOI: 10.1109/LSP.2012.2185492.

[10] Huang S and Yang J. Unitary Regression Classification with Total Minimum Projection Error for Face Recognition. IEEE Signal Processing Letters, 20 (5), pp. 443-446, 2013. DOI: 10.1109/LSP.2013.2250957.

[11] Huang S and Yang J. Kernel Linear Regression for Low Resolution Face Recognition Under Variable Illumination. In Proc. of IEEE International Conf. on Acoustics, Speech and Signal Processing, pp. 1945-1948, 2012. DOI: 10.1109/ICASSP.2012.6288286

[12] Dornaika F, Traboulsi YE and Assoum A. Adaptive Two Phase Sparse Representation Classifier for Face Recognition. In Proc. of International Conference on Advanced Concepts for Intelligent Vision Systems, Springer, p. 182-191, 2013. DOI: 10.1007/978-3-319-02895-8_64.

[13] Liao S, Jain AK and Li SZ. Partial Face Recognition: Alignment-Free Approach. IEEE Trans. on Pattern Analysis and Machine Intelligence, 35 (5), pp. 1193-1205, 2013. DOI: 10.1109/TPAMI.2012.191

[14] Li X, Dai D, Zhang X and Ren C. Structured Sparse Error Coding for Face Recognition with Occlusion. IEEE Trans. on Image Processing. 22 (5), p. 1889-1900, 2013. DOI: 10.1109/TIP.2013.2237920.

[15] Bonnen K, Klare BF, and Jain AK. Component-based Representation in

Automated Face Recognition. IEEE Trans. on Information Forensics and Security, 8(1), 239-253, 2013. DOI: 10.1109/TIFS.2012.2226580.

[16] Gonzalez-Sosa E, Vera-Rodriguez R, Fierrez J, and Ortega-Garcia, J. Dealing with Occlusions in Face Recognition by Region-based Fusion. In Proc. of 2016 IEEE International Carnahan Conference on Security Technology (ICCST), p. 1-6, October 2016. DOI: 10.1109/CCST.2016.7815707

[17] Min R, Hadid A, and Dugelay JL. Efficient Detection of Occlusion Prior to Robust Face Recognition. The Scientific World Journal, 2014. DOI: 10.1155/2014/519158.

[18] Tan X, Chen S, Zhou ZH, and Liu J. Face Recognition under Occlusions and Variant Expressions with Partial Similarity. IEEE Transactions on Information Forensics and Security, 4 (2), p. 217-230, 2009. DOI: 10.1109/TIFS.2009.2020772.

[19] Min R, Hadid A, and Dugelay JL. Improving the Recognition of Faces Occluded by Facial Accessories. In Proc. of IEEE International Conference on Automatic Face and Gesture Recognition Workshops (FG 2011), p. 442-447, March 2011. DOI: 10.1109/FG.2011.5771439.

[20] Chou Y and Yang J. Partially-occluded Face Recognition Using Weighted Module Linear Regression Classification. In Proc. of IEEE International Symposium on Circuits and Systems, p. 578-581, 2016. DOI: 10.1109/ISCAS.2016.7527306.

[21] Zhang T, Li J, Jia W, Sun J, and Yang H. Fast and Robust Occluded Face Detection in ATM Surveillance, Pattern Recognition Letters, 107, p. 33–40, 2018. DOI: 10.1016/j.patrec.2017.09.011

[22] Dagnes N, Vezzetti E, Marcolin F, and Tornincasa S. Occlusion Detection and Restoration Techniques for 3D Face Recognition: A Literature Review. Machine Vision and Applications, 29(5), 789–813, 2018. DOI: 10.1007/s00138-018-0933-z

[23] Su Y, Yang Y, Guo Z, and Yang W. Face Recognition with Occlusion. In Proc. of IEEE Asian Conference on Pattern Recognition (ACPR), p. 670-674, November 2015. DOI: 10.1109/ACPR.2015.7486587.

[24] Ou W, You X, Tao D, Zhang P, Tang Y, and Zhu Z. Robust Face Recognition via Occlusion Dictionary Learning. Pattern Recognition, 47(4), 1559-1572, 2014. DOI: 10.1016/j.patcog.2013.10.017

[25] Mi JX, Su Y, and Lu J. Robust Face Recognition Based on Supervised Spare Representation. In Proc. of International Conference on Intelligent Computing (ICIC), 253-359, 2018. DOI: 10.1007/978-3-319-95957-3_28.

[26] Duan Y, Lu J, Feng J and Zhou J. Context-Aware Local Binary Feature Learning for Face Recognition. IEEE Transactions on Pattern Analysis and Machine Intelligence, 40(5), 1139 – 1153, 2018. DOI: 10.1109/TPAMI.2017.2710183.

[27] Duan Y, Lu J, Feng J. and Zhou J. Topology Preserving Structural Matching for Automatic Partial Face Recognition. IEEE Transactions on Information Forensics and Security. 13 (7), p. 1823-1837, 2018. DOI: 10.1109/TIFS.2018.2804919.

[28] Parkhi OM, Vedaldi A and Zisserman A. Deep Face Recognition. in Proc. of British Machine Vision Association Conference, 1, p. 1–12, 2015.

[29] Schroff F, Kalenichenko D and Philbin J. FaceNet: A Unified Embedding for Face Recognition and Clustering. in Proc. of IEEE Conference on Computer Vision and Pattern Recognition (CVPR), p. 815–823, 2015.

[30] Sun Y, Wang X, and Tang X. Deep Learning Face Representation from Predicting 10,000 Classes. in Proc. of CVPR, p. 1891–1898, 2014.

[31] Taigman Y, Yang M, Ranzato M, and Wolf L. DeepFace: Closing the Gap to Human-level Performance in Face Verification," In Proc. of CVPR, p. 1701–1708, 2014.

[32] Martinez A and Benavente R. The AR Face Database. Technical Report 24, Computer Vision Center (CVC) Barcelona .1998.

[33] Phillips PJ, Flynn PJ, Scruggs T, Bowyer KW, Chang J, Hoffman K, Marques J, Min J and Worek W. Overview of the Face Recognition Grand Challenge. In Proc. of IEEE Conference on Computer Vision and Pattern Recognition, vol. 1. San Diego, p. 947-954. 20–25 June 2005. DOI: 10.1109/CVPR.2005.268.

[34] He X and Niyogi P. Locality Preserving Projections. Advances in Neural Information Processing Systems, p. 153-160, 2004.

[35] X. He, Cai D, Yan S and Zhang HJ. Neighborhood Preserving Embedding. In Proc. of Tenth IEEE International Conference on Computer Vision. p. 1208-1213, 2005. DOI: 10.1109/ICCV.2005.167

[36] Flynn PJ. FRGC database v2.0 2003. http://bbs.beebiometrics.org/.

[37] Ahonen T, Hadid A and Pietikainen M. Face Description with Local Binary Patterns: Application to Face Recognition. IEEE Transactions on Pattern Analysis and Machine Intelligence, 28 (12), p. 2037-2041, Dec. 2006. DOI: 10.1109/TPAMI.2006.244.

[38] Ahonen T, Hadid A, and Pietikainen M. Face Description with Local Binary Patterns: Application to Face Recognition. IEEE Transactions on Pattern Analysis and Machine Intelligence, (12), p. 2037-2041, 2006. DOI: 10.1109/TPAMI.2006.244.

[39] Zafeiriou S, Zhang C, and Zhang Z. A Survey on Face Detection in the Wild: Past, Present and Future. Computer Vision and Image Understanding, 138, 1-24. 2015. DOI : 10.1016/j.cviu.2015.03.015.

[40] Wang Q. An Analysis of the Viola-Jones Face Detection Algorithm. Image Processing On Line, 4, p. 128-148, 2014. DOI: 10.5201/ipol.2014.104

[41] Zhang, K., Zhang, Z., Li, Z., & Qiao, Y. (2016). Joint face detection and alignment using multitask cascaded convolutional networks. IEEE Signal Processing Letters, 23 (10), 1499-1503. DOI: 10.1109/LSP.2016.2603342.

Chapter 6

Diffuse Optical Tomography System in Soft Tissue Tumor Detection

Umamaheswari Kumarasamy, G.V. Shrichandran and A. Vedanth Srivatson

Abstract

Topical review of recent trends in Modeling and Regularization methods of Diffuse Optical Tomography (DOT) system promotes the optimization of the forward and inverse modeling methods which provides a 3D cauterization at a faster rate of 40frames/second with the help of a laser torch as a hand-held device. Analytical, Numerical and Statistical methods are reviewed for forward and inverse models in an optical imaging modality. The advancement in computational methods is discussed for forward and inverse models along with Optimization techniques using Artificial Neural Networks (ANN), Genetic Algorithm (GA) and Artificial Neuro Fuzzy Inference System (ANFIS). The studies carried on optimization techniques offers better spatial resolution which improves quality and quantity of optical images used for morphological tissues comparable to breast and brain in Near Infrared (NIR) light. Forward problem is based on the location of sources and detectors solved statistically by Monte Carlo simulations. Inverse problem or closeness in optical image reconstruction is moderated by different regularization techniques to improve the spatial and temporal resolution. Compared to conventional methods the ANFIS structure of optimization for forward and inverse modeling provides early detection of Malignant and Benign tumor thus saves the patient from the mortality of the disease. The ANFIS technique integrated with hardware provides the dynamic 3D image acquisition with the help of NIR light at a rapid rate. Thereby the DOT system is used to continuously monitor the Oxy and Deoxyhemoglobin changes on the tissue oncology.

Keywords: Diffuse Optical Tomography (DOT), Near Infrared (NIR), Forward model, Inverse model, Regularization, Artificial Neural Networks (ANN), Genetic Algorithm (GA) and Artificial Neuro Fuzzy Inference System (ANFIS)

1. Introduction

A recent survey was taken in the UK, reported 4,884 deaths from a brain tumor and about 11,633 deaths from breast cancer. The tumor detection is complicated and earlier detection leads to better chances of effective treatment, thereby increasing the survival rate. In the last decade, the concept of imaging has raised by the discovery of the X- ray radiography technique. The imaging techniques are highly meant for diagnostic applications in medical field. Different parts of a body have different range of absorption level hence the penetration of propagating light photon level varies for each and every organ, whereas this is the major concept considered for imaging. The imaging trend started with the X- ray radiography [1], it provides a one-dimensional image of the bony structures in a photographic film which could give the visualization of bony defects and the soft tissue tracks are identified only after the administration of contrast agents or dyes. The advanced version of the X- ray radiography is the Digital Radiography system which also provides a single plane image and it has the additional features such as data collection system, processing, display and storage system. Here the data obtained can be stored in a memory for future use. The limitation is even after the dye usage only the large variations in soft tissues can be identified.

In X - ray computed tomography the imaging of the organ is done in various angles and the reconstruction is demonstrated mathematically over the computer and displayed on the monitor. For the soft tissue examination, the dye fluids are pumped into the ventricles for providing the variation or contrast in the image. Here the noise increases inherently over the square root of the dose as the dose must be increased to preserve the same amount of noise. Therefore, over dosage leads to the side effects such as skin allergy, then came the existence the nuclear imaging.

Nuclear Medical Imaging (NMI) [1] systems utilize the radioisotopes for imaging. The small amount of radioactive chemicals is injected into the arm vein or inhaled through, and then the amount of radioactivity of the organ is examined using the radiation detectors. NMI includes Emission Computed Tomography which displays the single plane slice of the object with radioactivity, insisting same as.

X - ray computed tomography. In Single Positron Emission Tomography, gamma camera is used to create a three-dimensional representation of the radioisotope injected organ. Positron Emission Tomography (PET) imaging provides the cross- sectional images of positron emitting isotopes, which demonstrate the biological function and even physiological and pathological characteristics. The injected radioisotope may create allergic reactions and it takes hours to get clear from the blood and it's a time-consuming process.

Magnetic Resonance Imaging (MRI) uses a magnetic field and high radio frequency signals to obtain anatomical information about the human body as cross-sectional images. The imaging technique needs the subject to be still while imaging, when there occurs a move and it blurs the output image. Radiations utilized here are highly ionized which causes harm and it is a tremendous time consuming and cost inefficient process for early tumor detection. The Ultrasonic imaging system is used for obtaining images of an almost entire range of internal organs in the abdomen. While it is completely reflected at boundaries with gas and there is a serious restriction in investigation of and through gas containing structures. The ultrasonic waves could not penetrate the bony structures hence imaging the brain is impossible.

Diffuse Optical Tomography (DOT) [2, 3] employs near infra-red light of range 700-1000 nm [4] which is non-invasive and non-ionizing radiation, therefore causes no harm or side effects. It has its main application of imaging the soft tissue organs such as the brain and breast for diagnosing tumor using the biological parameters [5, 6] such as oxygenation etc. The brain and breast tumor or lesion can be detected by examining the oxygenated, deoxygenated hemoglobin, water and lipids (proteins). DOT imaging [7] provides a number of advantages, such as reduced size setup in turn lead to portability, real-time imaging, low instrumental cost and less time consumption when compared to the other imaging techniques but is generally known to have a low image resolution which limits its further clinical application. **Table 1**: Compares Biomedical Imaging Modalities- Diffuse optical

Parameters	DOT	CT	MRI	PET
Cost	$150,000	$300,000	$1,000,000	$1,446,546
Imaging Time	15–20 mins	45–60 mins	45–70 mins	75–90 mins
Size	60 x 45 cm	50 x 50 cm	4x4m	25x36x17cm
Sensitivity	50%	90%	91%	93%
Specificity	100%	56%	71%	70%

Table 1.
Comparison of biomedical imaging modalities.

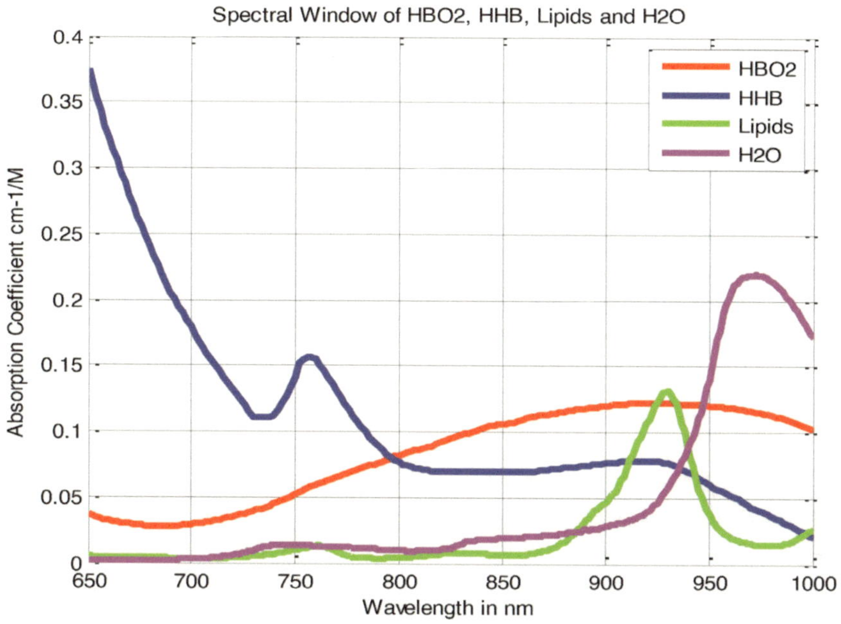

Figure 1.
Absorption spectra of deoxy-hemoglobin (Hb), oxy-hemoglobin (HbO_2), lipids and water.

tomography evaluated with Computer Tomography (CT), Magnetic Resonance Imaging (MRI), and Positron Emission Tomography (PET). The parameters namely cost, imaging time, size, sensitivity and specificity are compared.

The main absorbers of near-infrared (NIR) light in blood-perfused tissues are Oxy-hemoglobin, deoxyhemoglobin, Lipids (Bulk proteins) and water. NIR Spectral Window absorption spectra are between 650 and 1000 NM are shown in **Figure 1** is obtained from compiled absorption data for water [8] and hemoglobin [9]. Hence, light in this spectral window penetrates deeply into tissues, thus allowing for non-invasive investigations. The NIR light penetration depth into tissues is limited, by the hemoglobin absorption at shorter wavelengths and by the water absorption at longer wavelengths.

Different systems in DOT are Continuous Wave (CW) imaging [6], Time Domain (TD) and Frequency Domain (FD). Continuous imaging is the study of hemodynamic and oxygenation changes in superficial tissues. It requires a source of constant intensity modulated at low frequency. Measuring the intensity of light transmitted between two points on the surface of the tissue is economical. Optimum sensitivity is achieved by a number of distinct sources and detectors. Intensity measurements are sensitive and are unable to distinguish between the absorption and scattering effects. Time Domain (TD) system uses photon counting detectors, slow but highly sensitive. The temporal distribution of photons is produced in short duration. Short pulses of light are transmitted through a highly scattering medium known as a Temporal Point Spread Function (TPSF). Frequency Domain (FD) [9] system is relatively inexpensive, easy to develop and provides fast temporal sampling up to 50HZ.The system acquires quick measurements regarding the amplitude and phase of scattering and absorption in the frequency domain at high detected intensities.

2. Methods

2.1 Forward model

The NIR light propagates within the biological tissue in a turbid medium [5]. Light particles scatters with cell particles and the medium either absorbs or scatter the light. The positions and orientations of scatters are described by mesoscopic and macroscopic. In mesoscopic the particles in turbid media of dense concentration and light transport are modeled by Radiative Transport Equation (RTE) [3]. In macroscopic photon transport on mean free path, diffusion approximation holds good for turbid media. Therefore, the isotropic scattering effect and light transport within the tissues is described by the diffusion Equation.

2.1.1 Radiative transport equation

Light transport in tissues derived using RTE, assumes the energy particles do not change in collisions hence refractive index is constant with the medium [8]. RTE is used to describe anisotropic field and the photon propagation in tissue, is given by

$$\hat{s}.\nabla I(r,\omega,\hat{s}) + \left(\mu_a + \mu_s + \frac{i\omega}{c}\right) I(r,\omega,\hat{s}) = \mu_s \int f(\hat{s},\hat{s}') I(r,\omega,\hat{s}) d^2\hat{s}' + q(r,\omega,\hat{s}) \quad (1)$$

I(r, ω, $\hat{s}$) is radiance with modulation frequency ω at point r, in the direction $\hat{s}$. μ_a, μ_s are absorption and scattering coefficients respectively and c is the speed of light. The scattering phase function.

f ($\hat{s}$, $\hat{s}'$) is used to characterize the intensity of a beam, that is scattered from the direction $\hat{s}'$ into the direction $\hat{s}$. The scattering phase function commonly used Henyey - Greenstein scattering function.

$$f(\cos\theta) = \frac{1}{4\pi}\left[\frac{1-g^2}{(1+g^2-2g\cos\theta)^{3/2}}\right] \quad (2)$$

where θ is the angle between the two directions $\hat{s}$ and $\hat{s}$', and g is the anisotropy factor which is used to characterize the angular distribution of tissue scattering.

The fluence at point r modulation frequency ω and in the direction $\hat{s}$ is defined by

$$\varphi(r,\omega) = \int_{4\pi} I(r,\omega,\hat{s}) \quad (3)$$

The Monte Carlo Method is used to solve the radiative transfer Equation.

2.1.2 Diffusion approximation

The directional flux magnitude is less compared to isotropic fluence magnitude within the tissue. The light field 'diffuses' means the scattering interaction dominates over absorption. The diffusion equation [10] approximation is given as

$$-\nabla K(r)\nabla\varphi(r,\omega) + \left(\mu_a(r) + \frac{i\omega}{c(r)}\right)\varphi(r,\omega) = q_0(r,\omega) \tag{4}$$

$\mu a(r)$ absorption coefficient, $q_0(r,\omega)$ is isotropic source, $\Phi(\text{r},\omega)$ is photon influence rate with modulation frequency ω at position r. The velocity of light in medium c(r) at any point r is defined as $c_0/n\ (r)$ where c_0 is the speed of light in vacuum, n(r) is the index of refraction.

Diffusion coefficient is described as

$$K(r) = \frac{1}{3\left[\mu_a(r) + \mu_s'(r)\right]} \tag{5}$$

Where the reduced scattering coefficient is $\mu s'(r) = \mu s(r)\ [1 - g(r)]$, g(r) is anisotropy factor. The refractive index mismatch at the tissue boundary is eluded by applying Robin boundary condition (type III). Eq. (5) solved using Finite Element Method (FEM) which provides stable solution [11].

3. Modeling techniques

3.1 Analytical model

Analytical model has fast computation and the Green's function is applied for modeling the diffusion equation or RTE analysis. The Green's function provides a solution when the source is a spatial and temporal function. It is commonly used to solve the forward problem for image reconstruction, specifically for fast imaging techniques. Optical properties are modeled by a green's function [3] for a slab representing the homogeneous background; with an additional perturbation term represent the spherical insertion.

3.2 Statistical model

Models the individual photon with Poisson error incorporated in the model. Monte Carlo method is a gold standard statistical technique in diffuse optics. The geometry of the model is defined by μ_a, μ_s, the refractive index and the photon trajectories. Light propagation in non- diffusive domains is calculated by Monte Carlo techniques. Random walk theory provides a distinct approach in which photon transport is modeled as a series of steps on the discrete cubic lattice. Random walk theory [9] is particularly suited to model time-domain measurements. The random walk extension technique has been developed for modeling media with anisotropic optical properties, maintaining the cubic lattice.

3.3 Numerical model

Numerical techniques have the potential for modeling complex geometries. Finite Element Method (FEM) [8] is used to represent the inhomogeneous distribution [12] of optical properties in an arbitrary geometry. Boundary Element

Method (BEM) [3], Finite Difference Method (FDM) and Finite Volume Method (FVM) are applied in more specialized applications. Finite Element Method divides the reconstruction domain into finite element meshes. The optimal computational efficiency of FEM depends on the smallest number of elements to represent the internal field by a finite element mesh. Adaptively refine the mesh by placing more elements when the field changes rapidly.

4. Regularization

The ill-condition inverse problem [5] in image reconstruction provides poor localization of imaging in localized or sparse regions. To overcome the ill posed problem in inverse model, regularization is applied in inverse model. The various forms of regularization are standard/Tikhonov regularization, exponential/spatial regularization, generalized least mean square regularization, adaptive regularization and model-based regularization [8, 11, 13–15].

4.1 Standard regularization

Standard regularization [16] or constant regularization is of Tikhonov type. Here the regularization is based on the already available information that may be the noise characteristics [11] or structural information [17] of the data, more prior information [13] usage leads to a better outcome of reconstruction procedure or robustness to the noise in the data.

$$P(\mu_a) = \lambda_T \|\mu_a\|^2 \tag{6}$$

λ is a regularization parameter (i.e.) constant chosen to stabilize the solution and its value varies from 1e-6 to 10.

$$\lambda_T = (\sigma_y)^2 / (\sigma_{\mu-\mu_0})^2 \tag{7}$$

The ill posed problem with inverse model is solved by adding the penalty term to the objective function.

$$\Omega = \|y - G(\mu_a)\|^2 + P(\mu_a) \tag{8}$$

y = ln (A) is the measured experimental data here A specifies the amplitude, G (μ_a) modeled data and penalty term is P(μ_a) removes the high frequency components. Iteratively linearization minimizes "Ω" by $\frac{\partial \Omega}{\partial \mu a} = 0$. Using Taylor series of expansion Tikhonov minimization is obtained by

$$\Omega = \|y - G(\mu_a)\|^2 + \lambda_T \|L(\mu_a - \mu_0)\|^2 \tag{9}$$

L is the dimensionless matrix and μ_0 is prior estimate. The penalty term minimization scheme along with linearization leads to the updated equation (Gauss-Newton update equation)

$$[J^T J + \lambda I] \nabla \mu_a = J(y - G(\mu_a) \tag{10}$$

'J' is a Jacobian ∂G (μ_a) / ∂ (μ_a) gives the rate of change with modeled data with respect to μ_a and I represent the Identity matrix. The diffuse optical tomography inverse problem sets a least square problem, which is solved by matching experimentally measured boundary data with modeled data iteratively.

Linearization of the as in (7) leads to an updated equation.

$$\left[J^T J - \lambda L^T L\right] = J^T \delta_{i-1} - \lambda_T L^T L(\mu_{i-1} - \mu_0) \tag{11}$$

The δ_{i-1} represents data misfit model and T for transpose operation. The resolution provided by as in (9) concentrates more on the detected position.

4.2 Adaptive regularization

In adaptive regularization [15] the regularization parameter λ varies with respect to the projection error [18]. Projection error Φ is defined as the difference in measured data in the modeled data which is expressed as in (12).

$$\nabla\varphi = |y - G(\mu_a)|^2 \tag{12}$$

The regularization parameter λ is denoted as

$$\lambda = 1/\left(2 + e^{-\Delta\varphi}\right) \tag{13}$$

The regularization parameter λ varies in the range from 1/3 to 1/2. As in (13) 'e' represents the exponential function and ΔΦ representing the change in projection error. A penalty term for projection error-based regularization is expressed as

$$P(\mu_a) = \lambda(\Delta\varphi)\|\mu_a\|^2 \tag{14}$$

Linearization leads to an updated equation.

$$\Delta\mu = J^T\left[JJ^T + \lambda JJ^T I\right]^{-1}\varphi \tag{15}$$

As in Eq. (15) Δμ represents the change in absorption coefficient. Projection error determines the accuracy, while JJ^T is denoted as the Hessian matrix with diagonal elements.

4.3 Exponential regularization

Exponential regularization is otherwise called as spatially varying regularization [14] or wavelength chromophore specific regularization, which is based on the physics of the problem. This simplicity makes it widely used for solving inverse problems especially in the cases where the prior information is not available. λ(r) is spatially varying regularization parameter, where r represents the position spatially. The spatial variation is attained by an exponential function in the form

$$\lambda(r) = \lambda_e\, exp\,(r/R)\lambda_c \tag{16}$$

As in (16) the radius of imaging domain is R, λ_c, λ_e are the regularization parameters at the edge and center of the location. The spatially varying regularization has exponential term with low value at the center and large value near the boundary of the imaging domain in-order to neutralize the hypersensitivity near the boundary, which appears due to detectors located at the boundary. In order to determine the regularization parameter λ(r), the generalized objective function is given as,

$$\Omega = \|y - G(\mu)\|^2 + \lambda(r)\|L(\mu - \mu_0)\|^2 \tag{17}$$

As in (17) L is a dimensionless regularization matrix and μ_0 is the prior estimate the of properties, while the penalty term for exponential regularization is represented as

$$P(\mu_a) = \lambda(r)\|\mu_a\|^2 \tag{18}$$

Linearizing (17) leads to a Jacobian updated equation as

$$[J^T J - \lambda(r)L^T L] = J^T \delta_{i-1} - \lambda(r)L^T L(\mu_{i-1} - \mu_0) \tag{19}$$

Exponential Regularization captures the hessian matrix diagonal as $J^T J$.

4.4 Model based regularization

Model based regularization utilizes the combination of model resolution matrix [19] and data resolution matrix. The objective is to match the modeled data with the observed data. By this method of regularization, the spatial resolution of the reconstructed image is improved [18].

$$y = G(\mu_a) \tag{20}$$

Expanding using Taylor series gives the equation

$$y = G(\mu_a) = G(\mu_{a0}) + G'(\mu_a)(\mu_a - \mu_{a0}) + (\mu_a - \mu_{a0})^T G''(\mu_a)(\mu_a - \mu_{a0}) + \dots \tag{21}$$

Jacobian matrix $J = G'(\mu_a)$ and Hessian matrix $H = G''(\mu_a)$.
Linearizing (21) then

$$y = G(\mu_{a0}) + J(\mu_a - \mu_{a0}) \tag{22}$$

using $y - G(\mu_{a0}) = \delta$ and $\Delta\mu_a = \mu_a - \mu_{a0}$ [20].

$$\text{Updated equation } \delta = J\Delta\tilde{\mu}_a \tag{23}$$

Change in absorption coefficient ($\Delta\mu_a$) is derived as in (18) as

$$\Delta\mu_a = [J^T J + \lambda I]^{-1} J^T J \Delta\tilde{\mu}_a \tag{24}$$

In the case of $\lambda = 0$

$$\Delta\mu_a = \Delta\tilde{\mu}_a \tag{25}$$

Regularization term is linearized using the model resolution matrix, which depends on the forward model and regularization but not on data. Because of the ill posed nature of the problem as in (25) $\lambda > 0$, then

$$\Delta\mu_a \neq \Delta\tilde{\mu}_a \tag{26}$$

As in Eq. (24) leads to a model resolution matrix.

$$M = \left[J^T J + \lambda I\right]^{-1} J^T J \tag{27}$$

As in (27) M has the dimension of NN x NN and it purely depends on J^TJ and the regularization term used. Linearization of as in (27) leads to an updated Jacobian matrix. λ varies from 0 to 1.

$$\left[J^T J + c\lambda_i I\right]\Delta\mu_a = J^T\left(y - G(\mu_a)\right) \tag{28}$$

The regularization parameter of a model resolution matrix is given as

$$\lambda_{im} = M_{ii}/\, max\,(M_{ii})\ \text{for i} = 1, 2, \ \ldots\ldots\ldots\ \text{NN} \tag{29}$$

The model resolution matrix can be applied for deriving the linearization as in (26) for both constant and spatially varying regularization parameters. The matrix varies for constant and spatially varying regularization. The model resolution matrix main aim is to provide the better resolution characteristics without depending on data.

The data resolution matrix concentrates only on the data not on the image characteristics [21]. It defines that how well the estimated $\Delta\mu a$ fits the observed data, hence it is important to consider data too in order to improve the resolution characteristics.

$$J\Delta\mu_a = \delta' \tag{30}$$

Data resolution matrix is derived using the Jacobian matrix (J) and the regularization technique which is used for reconstruction. It is evaluated by matching the predicted data with the obtained data [22].

$$\delta' = y - G(\mu_{a0}) \tag{31}$$

The data-resolution matrix does not depend on a specific data (y) or error in it but are exclusively the properties of J and the regularization (λ) used. The closer it is to the identity matrix, the smaller are the prediction errors for δ, where δ\` as in (31) representing the data misfit.

Data resolution matrix D is given as

$$D = J^T J\left[JJ^T + \lambda I\right]^{-1} \tag{32}$$

Linearizing (31) leads to an updated equation

$$\Delta\mu_i = J^T\left[JJ^T + \lambda I\right]^{-1}\delta_{i-1} \tag{33}$$

The regularization parameter of a data resolution matrix is given as

$$\lambda_{id} = D_{ii}/\, max\,(D_{ii})\ \text{for i} = 1, 2, \ \ldots\ldots\ldots\ \text{NN} \tag{34}$$

As in (26) and as in (34) the regularization parameter of the model-based regularization λ_i is given as

$$\lambda_i = (\lambda_{im} + \lambda_{id})/2 \tag{35}$$

Penalty term for the regularization scheme is given as

$$P(\mu_a) = c\lambda_i \|\mu_a\|^2 \quad (36)$$

Where c provides the weight for penalty term and it is a constant term.

5. Inverse model

Newton - Raphson iterative method to find the optical parameter μ_a, μ_s by solving the minimum objective function.

$$\psi(\mu) = |\varphi^m - \varphi^c|^2 + \lambda|\mu - \mu_0|^2 \quad (37)$$

Φ_m and Φ_c are calculated and measured radiance at the detectors. λ is regularization parameter, μ, μ_0 are current and initial estimates of optical properties at each node.

The initial values of absorption and scattering properties were estimated homogenously [23]. Update Φoptical distribution in Tikhonov Regularization is given by Eq. (39).

$$\mu = J^T\left(JJ^T + \lambda H_{\max} I\right)^{-1}(\varphi_m - \varphi_c) \quad (38)$$

$\Delta\mu$ Optical parameter update vector, H_{max} maximum main diagonal element value of the matrix JJ^T. J is Jacobian matrix for inverse problem plots the variation in log amplitude and phase for both absorption and diffusion modification in every node.

5.1 Jacobian reduction

Jacobian matrix J has the size as number of measurements NM by the number of FEM nodes NN i.e. NM x NN is calculated using ad joint method. Limit the Jacobian [23, 24] to the measured amplitude data and optical absorption. Jacobian links a change in log amplitude, at the boundary with a change in absorption coefficient μ_a.

$$J = \begin{bmatrix} \dfrac{\partial \ln I_1}{\partial \mu_{a1}} & \cdots & \dfrac{\partial \ln I1}{\partial \mu_{aNN}} \\ \vdots & \ddots & \vdots \\ \dfrac{\partial \ln I_{NM}}{\partial \mu_{a1}} & \cdots & \dfrac{\partial \ln I_1}{\partial \mu_{aNN}} \end{bmatrix} \quad (39)$$

The size of the Jacobian matrix is reduced by calculating the total sensitivity throughout the imaging domain and a new Jacobian $\tilde{Jij}$ is formed [25].

$$\tilde{J}_{ij} = \begin{cases} J_{ij} \text{ if } \sum_{i=1}^{NM} J_{ij} \geq threshold \\ 0 \text{ if } \sum_{i=1}^{NM} J_{ij} < threshold \end{cases} \quad (40)$$

'j' corresponds to a node number within the domain. Reduction of Jacobian matrix improves the computational speed and efficiency of image reconstruction.

5.2 Bayesian framework

Ill posed condition of DOT problem, the solution is robust. To overcome this problem a priori information is incorporated constraint in the space of unknowns. Bayesian approach proposes an algorithm for spatial physiological prior [26]. High resolution anatomical image is segmented into sub-images. Each image is assigned a mean value with a prior probability density function of the image. 'Confidence level' is defined in the form of an image variance formulation to allow local variations within sub-images. MAP (Maximum a posteriori) estimates of the image [26, 27] is formed based on the formulation of the image's probability density function.

$$\hat{y}_{MAP} = argmax\{\,log\, p(y/x) + log\, p(x)\} \tag{41}$$

p(y/x) is log likelihood function; p(x) is a probability density function.

Alternating minimization algorithm sequentially updates the unknown parameters, solves the optimization problem. Probability density function of the ith sub-image is defined in the spatial prior as

$$p(x_i/\sigma_i) = \frac{1}{\left(2\prod \sigma_i^2\right)^{N_i}/2}\, exp\left(\frac{-1}{2\sigma_i^2}|X_i - C_i|^2\right), i = 1, 2. \ldots M \tag{42}$$

M is number of sub regions, N_i is number of voxels in the ith sub image, x_i is the unknown sub image, C_i is chromosphere mean concentration, σ_i^2 is single variance.

The confidence level is incorporated into the statistical reconstruction procedure, the sub-image variance.

$$p(\sigma_i) = \frac{1}{\left(2\prod \gamma_i^2\right)^{N_i/2}}\, exp\left(-\frac{1}{2\gamma_i^2}|\sigma_i - \sigma_j|^2\right), i = 1, 2, \ldots M \tag{43}$$

γ_i is the variance and $\sigma_{i'}$ is the mean value of σ_i.

6. Experimental set-up

The practical setup of image acquisition as shown in **Figure 2** includes optical components, electrical components, control, data acquisition and image reconstruction [28].

The optical Multiplexer has three parts namely the motor, drive and Black box (PMT) Photon multiplier tube. Driver rotates the optical multiplexer to guide the energy to PMT, which converts light to electrical signals. The signal is amplified by an Amplifier and preprocessed electrical signals are given to Data acquisition card. Data acquisition software samples the raw data, post process and controls the hardware. The personal computer delivers commands to alter the fiber switch (source channel) sequentially. 16 X 16 input and output fibers constitutes to 256 sources – detector pairs. Image is reconstructed using inverse modeling such as Jacobian reduction with FEM.

The optical Multiplexer has three parts namely the motor, drive and Black box (PMT) Photon multiplier tube. Driver rotates the optical multiplexer to guide the

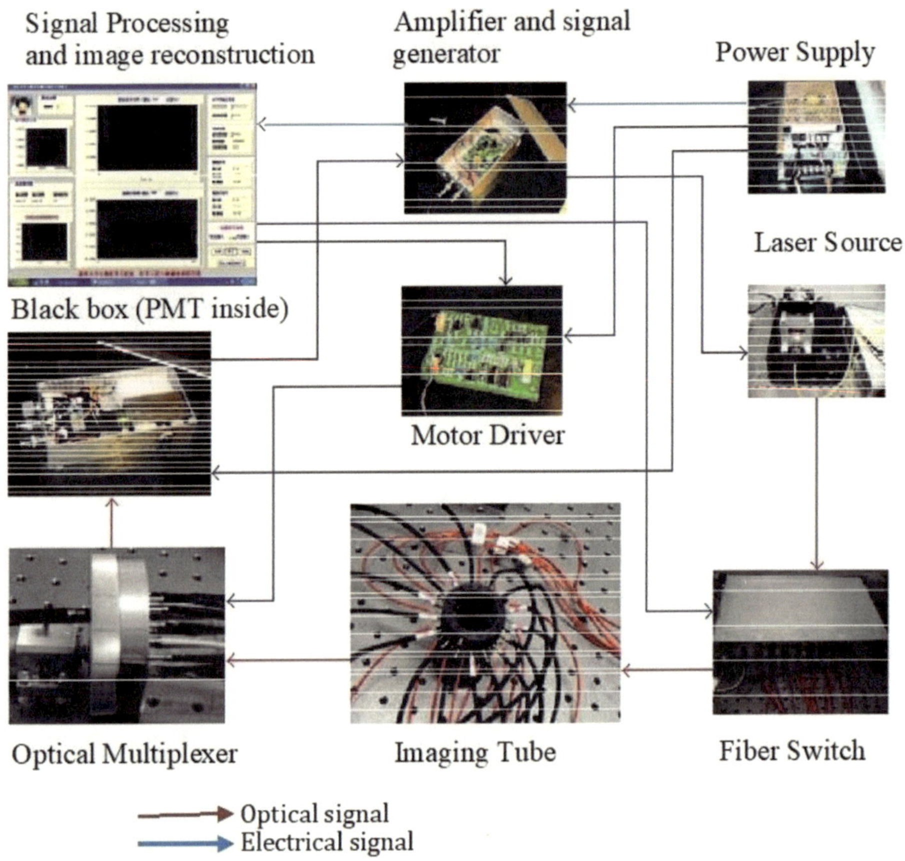

Figure 2.
The practical imaging system.

energy to PMT, which converts light to electrical signals. The signal is amplified by an Amplifier and preprocessed electrical signals are given to Data acquisition card. Data acquisition software samples the raw data, post process and controls the hardware. The personal computer delivers commands to alter the fiber switch (source channel) sequentially. 16 X 16 input and output fibers constitutes to 256 sources – detector pairs. Image is reconstructed using inverse modeling such as Jacobian reduction with FEM.

7. Optimization techniques

7.1 Artificial neural networks

Artificial Neural Network (ANN) is data structure accurately approximates a nonlinear relationship between a set of input and output parameters. It maps the input optical properties for spatial frequency domain in inverse modeling. Perform Monte Carlo simulation and fit it to ANN to output the data. Neural Network is trained to predict the tissue reflectance for strongly and weakly absorbing media.

The parallel Back propagation neural network distinguishes nonlinear relationship between spatial location of tumors and light intensity around the boundary of the tissue [29]. The neural network is trained for fast reconstruction in diffuse optical tomography. Location and spacing of optical sources and detectors are optimized using neural network. To improve the resolution of DOT images in inverse model Fixed Grid Wavelet Network [30] image segmentation is applied to extract a smooth boundary in tumor images.

7.2 Genetic algorithm

Reconstruction of optical in homogeneities embedded in turbid medium using diffuse optical tomography. The optimization problem is solved by using genetic algorithm minimizing objective function [31, 32]. This approach is applied for full non- linear range of quantitative reconstruction. Crosstalk near the source detector artifacts are the major inaccuracies in diffuse optical tomography images [33]. This problem can be solved by a global optimization method namely genetic algorithm for estimating the optical parameters.

7.3 Adaptive neuro fuzzy interference system

Adaptive Neuro fuzzy Inference system can be used for optical imaging, solving the non-linear ill posed problem with accurate qualitative and quantitative optical image reconstruction. The proposed method using ANFIS architecture will provide fast and accurate optical image reconstruction hence can achieve classification accuracy, volume and the layer thickness measurement of tumor.

8. Simulation techniques

The simulation software for modeling diffuse optical tomography is CULA, NIRFAST NETGEN and MIMICS. CULA is GPU Accelerated Linear Algebra which has a parallel computing architecture to dramatically improve the computation speed of sophisticated mathematics and also contains routines for systems solvers, singular value decompositions and Eigen problems. For reconstruction in diffuse optical tomography it facilitates singular value decomposition, matrix multiplication, matrix inversion etc.

NIRFAST is Near Infrared Fluorescence and Spectroscopy Tomography [33, 34] which is an FEM based software package designed for modeling Near Infrared Frequency domain [35] light transport in tissue.

NETGEN [36] is an automatic 3D tetrahedral mesh generator which accepts input from Constructive Solid Geometry (CSG) or Boundary Representation (BR) from the STL (Stereo Lithography) file format. It contains modules for mesh optimization and hierarchical mesh refinement and it is also open-source software available for Unix/Linux and Windows.

MIMICS is software specially developed for medical image processing. The ROI (Region of Interest) is selected in the segmentation process which is converted to a 3D surface model using an adapted marching cubes algorithm that takes the partial volume effect into account, leading to very accurate 3D model. The 3D files are represented in the STL format.

9. Conclusion

The Diffuse Optical Tomography (DOT) imaging experimental setup has three kinds of noise namely thermal noise, shot noise and relatively intensity noise. The shot noise from dark current of photodetector has Poisson statistics, solved by using Bayesian network in inverse problem. DOT has undetermined problem due less measured data in the forward model compared to the pixels reconstructed in inverse model. The forward problem solved by FEM and regularization techniques to improve the spatial resolution of DOT images. Diffuse Optical Tomography (DOT) has significant advancement since it becomes faster, more robust, less susceptible to error, and able to acquire data at a number of wavelengths with more source–detector combinations. Images reconstructed in 3D, uses more sophisticated techniques, which can be adapted by incorporating prior information and by compensating for some of the unavoidable sources of measurement error. DOT imaging is still a laboratory-based technique, yet to progress to develop a handheld for detection of tumor in morphological tissues in clinical applications. Qualitative and quantitative accuracy has to be improved in DOT, both of which are limited by poor spatial resolution. Improved image quality is achievable by adopting the optimization techniques namely Artificial Neural Networks, Genetic Algorithm and Adaptive Neuro Fuzzy Inference System. Enhancement of DOT can also achieve higher performance using multimodal imaging techniques. DOT is as a low-cost, portable imaging system to be developed at the bedside. The best modeling and reconstruction methods provide an ideal DOT instrumentation.

Acknowledgements

The research was carried out in Department of Electronics and Communication and Department of Mechanical Engineering in SRM TRP Engineering College, Trichy, Tamil Nadu, India. We express our gratitude to our management, faculty and research scholars in SRM TRP Engineering College, Trichy, Tamil Nadu, India, who provided skill and proficiency that completely helped in the development of an optimized DOT instrument for detection of sarcoma cells. We are very grateful to Radiation Oncology Centre at Trichy SRM Medical College Hospital & Research Centre, Tiruchirappalli for providing the insights on tumor detection.

Conflicts of interest

Our project promotes the social awareness on early tumor detection at cellular level. Diffuse Optical Tomography (DOT) provides harmless non-invasive detection of tumor cells. Today around 70% of people are suffering from sarcoma in soft tissue. Detection at earlier stage helps the patient for early diagnosis and prevents them from clinical pathology. We are interested to promote our review based on diffuse optical tomography instrumentation without any conflicts of interest as review article.

Compliance with ethical standards

1. Disclosure of potential conflicts of interests.

2. Conflict of Interest: The authors declare that they have no conflict of interest.

3. Research involving human participants and/ or animals.

4. Ethical approval: "This chapter does not contain any studies with human participants or animals performed by any of the authors."

Author details

Umamaheswari Kumarasamy[1*], G.V. Shrichandran[2] and A. Vedanth Srivatson[1]

1 Department of Electronics and Communication Engineering, SRM TRP Engineering College, Trichy, Tamil Nadu, India

2 Department of Computer Science Engineering, SRM Institute of Science and Technology, Chennai, Tamil Nadu, India

*Address all correspondence to: umaragsug@gmail.com

References

[1] John G. Webster 2003: Medical Instrumentation Application and Design Wiley Third edition. DOI:10.1097/00004669-197807000-00017

[2] S. L. Jacques and B. W. Pogue 2008: Tutorial on diffuse light transport J. Biomed. Opt., 13, 04130. https://doi.org/10.1117/1.2967535

[3] A. Gibson, J. C. Hebden, and S. R. Arridge 2005: Recent advances in diffuse optical tomography Phys. Med. Bio. 50, R1–R43. https://doi.org/10.1117/1.2967535

[4] S. R. Arridge 1999: Optical tomography in medical imaging Inverse Probl., 15, R41–R93. https://doi.org/10.1007/978-94-010-0975-1_17

[5] S. R. Arridge and J. C. Hebden 1997: Optical imaging in medicine: II. Modelling and reconstruction Phys. Med.Biol. 42, 841–853. DOI: 10.1088/0031-9155/42/5/008

[6] H. Dehghani, S. Srinivasan, B. W. Pogue, and A. Gibson 2009: Numerical modelling and image reconstruction in diffuse optical tomography Phil. Trans. R. Soc.,A 367, 3073–3093. doi: 10.1098/rsta.2009.0090

[7] A. Gibson and H. Dehghani 2009: Diffuse optical imaging Phil. Trans. R. Soc., A 367, 3055–3072. doi: 10.1098/rsta.2009.0080

[8] Hale, G. M., and M. R. Querry 1973: Optical Constants of Water in the 200 nm to 200 μm Wavelength Region, Appl. Opt. 12, 555-563. https://doi.org/10.1364/AO.12.000555

[9] http://omlc.ogi.edu/spectra/hemoglobin/summary.html.

[10] K.Uma Maheswari, S. Sathiyamoorthy, 2016: Soft tissue optical property extraction for carcinoma cell detection in diffuse optical tomography system under boundary element condition, OPTIK 127 (2016) 1281-1290. https://doi.org/10.1016/j.ijleo.2015.10.100

[11] Michael Chu, Karthik Vishwanath, A.D Klose and Hamid Dehghani 2009: Light transport in biological tissue using three - dimensional frequency-domain simplified spherical harmonics equations Phys Med Biol.2009 Apr 21; 54 (8): 2493-509. doi: 10.1088/0031-9155/54/8/016

[12] K. UmaMaheswari, S. Sathiyamoorthy, G. Lakshmi, 2016: Numerical solution for image reconstruction in diffuse optical tomography, journal of engineering and applied sciences Vol.11, No.2, pp. 1332-1336.www.arpnjournals.org / Jeas/research_papers/rp_2016/jeas_0116_3501.Pdf

[13] M. Schweiger, S. R. Arridge, M. Hiroaka, and D. T. Delpy 1995: The finite element model for the propagation of light in scattering media: Boundary and source conditions Med. Phys., 22, 1779–1792. doi: 10.1118/1.597634

[14] S. R. Arridge and M. Schweiger 1995: Photon- measurement density functions. Part 2: Finite-element-method calculations Appl. Opt., 34, 8026–8037. https://doi.org/10.1364/AO.34.008026

[15] M. Guven, B. Yazici, X. Intes, and B. Chance 2005: Diffuse optical tomography with a priori anatomical information Phys. Med. Biol., 50, 2837–2858. https://doi.org/10.1117/12.479799

[16] B. W. Pogue, T. McBride, J. Prewitt, U. L. Osterberg, and K. D. Paulsen 1999: Spatially variant regularization improves diffuse optical tomography Appl. Opt., 38, 2950–2961. https://doi.org/10.1364/AO.38.002950

[17] H. Niu, P. Guo, L. Ji, Q. Zhao, and T. Jiang 2008: Improving image quality of diffuse optical tomography with a projection-error based adaptive regularization method Opt. Express 16, 12423–12434. https://doi.org/10.1364/OE.16.012423

[18] P. K. Yalavarthy, B. W. Pogue, H. Dehghani, and K.D. Paulsen 2007: Weight-matrix structured regularization provides optimal generalized least-squares estimate in diffuse optical tomography Med. Phys., 34, 2085–2098. doi: 10.1118/1.2733803

[19] R. Sukanyadevi, K. Umamaheswari, S. Sathiyamoorthy, 2013: Resolution improvement in diffuse optical tomography, IJCA ICIIIOES(9),3741.https://www.ijcaonline.orgproceedings/iciiioes/number9/14347-1656

[20] F.Larusson, S.Fantini and E. L Miller 2011: Hyperspectral image reconstruction for diffuse optical tomography Biomed. Opt. Express, 2, 946–965. doi: 10.1364/BOE.2.000946

[21] Deepak Karkala and Phaneendra K. Yalavarthya 2012: Data-resolution based optimization of the data -collection strategy for near infrared diffuse optical tomography Med. Phys. 39 (8). DOI: 10.1118/1.4736820

[22] P. K. Yalavarthy, B. W. Pogue, H. Dehghani, C. M. Carpenter, S. Jiang and K. D. Paulsen 2007: Structural information within regularization matrices improves near infrared diffuse optical tomography Opt.Express,15, 8043–8058. https://doi.org/10.1364/OE.15.008043

[23] S. H. Katamreddy, P. K. Yalavarthy 2012: Model-resolution based regularization improves near infrared diffuse optical tomography J. Opt. Soc. Am. A, Vol. 29, No. 5. https://doi.org/10.1364/JOSAA.29.000649

[24] Ville Kolehmainen 2001: Computational Methods for Light Transport in Optical Tomography Ph.D. thesis Kuopio University Publications C. Natural and Environmental Sciences, p.125. https://citeseerx.ist.psu.edu/viewdoc/download?doi=10.1.1.97.1872&rep=rep1&type=pdf

[25] Athanasios D. Zacharopoulos, Martin Schweiger, Ville Kolehmainen and Simon Arridge 2009: 3D shape based reconstruction of experimental data in Diffuse Optical Tomography Optics Express, Vol. 17, Issue 21, pp. 18940-18956 . DOI: 10.1088/0031-9155/49/12/n01

[26] C. S. Musgrove 2007: Issues related to the forward problem for endoscopic near-infrared diffuse optical tomography Thesis submitted to the Faculty of the Graduate College of Oklahoma State University, December. https://hdl.handle.net/11244/10248

[27] Intes X, Maloux C, Guven M, Yazici B, Chance B 2004: Diffuse optical tomography with physiological and spatial a priori constraints Phys Med Biol.,p 49(12):N155-63. doi: 10.1088/0031-9155/49/12/n01

[28] Huacheng Feng, Jing Bai, Xiaolei Song, Gang Hu, and Junjie Yao 2007: A Near-Infrared Optical Tomography System Based on Photomultiplier Tube International Journal of Biomedical Imaging Volume, 9 pages doi:10.1155/2007/28387

[29] Yudovsky D, Durkin AJ 2011: Spatial frequency domain spectroscopy of two layer media J Biomed Opt. Oct;16 (10):107005. https://doi.org/10.1364/OE.17.018940

[30] UmaMaheswari, K, Sathiyamoorthy, S, 2018:Fixed grid wavelet network segmentation on diffuse optical tomography image to detect sarcoma, Journal of Applied Research and Technology, Vol.16(2), pp.126-139. *doi*: 10.1109/42.918473

[31] Lizeng Sheng 2004: Finite Element Analysis and Genetic Algorithm Optimization Design for the Actuator Placement on a Large Adaptive Structure publisher *Blacksburg, Va.*: University Libraries, Virginia Polytechnic Institute and State University.https://vtechworks.lib.vt.edu/handle/ 10919/30184

[32] Behnoosh Tavakoli, Quing Zhu 2013: Two-step reconstruction method using global optimization and conjugate gradient for ultrasound-guided diffuse optical tomography J. Biomed. Opt. p.18 (1), 016000. https://doi.org/10.1117/1.JBO.18.1.016006

[33] Kwangmoo Koh, Seungjean Kim, Stephen Boyd, l1 ls 2008: A Matlab Solver for Large-Scale ℓ1-Regularized Least Squares Problems. https://web.stanford.edu/~boyd/l1_ls/l1_ls_usrguide.pdf

[34] https://wiki.thayer.dartmouth.edu/.

[35] Dehghani H, Eames ME, Yalavarthy PK, Davis SC, Srinivasan S, Carpenter CM, et al. Near infrared optical tomography using NIRFAST: Algorithms for numerical model and image reconstruction. algorithms Commun. Numer. Methods Eng. 2009; **25**:711-732. DOI: 10.1002/cnm.1162

[36] www.hpfem.jku.at/netgen